SO FAR, SO GOOD
THE AUTOBIOGRAPHY OF PAUL J. POLKA

Paul J. Polka

This book is dedicated to my loving wife, Joan,
who has put up with me for close to half a century.

Acknowledgements

Thanks to my wife, Joan, for her moral support during difficult times.

Thanks to my editor, Bridget Casterline, the hardest worker of the whole vast editorial staff.

Thanks to Dave Casterline for scanning the photos that went into the book.

Thanks to Brian Polka for showing what entrepreneurship is all about.

Thanks to Mickey Polka for helping to expand USA space exploration.

Thanks to Jimmy Polka for helping to keep our train system "on track."

Thanks to "Coop" for making me believe in Superman.

Thanks to "The Captain" for his wise, technical leadership.

Thanks to Doug Scott for watching my back at ejection seat meetings.

Thanks to Colonel Baker for letting me do my job without asking too many questions.

Thanks to Amy for teaching me to talk after a stroke.

Thanks to Sister Agnes for seeing in me what I didn't see in myself.

Thanks to Hazel for watching out for "The Kid" in the Air Force.

He was born with the gift of laughter
and a sense that the world was mad.

Rafael Sabatini, *Scaramouche*

Contents

Preface

I am not a writer, a fact that will no doubt become abundantly clear to you shortly.

I am a 77-year-old man who has had two strokes, stage 4 kidney disease, sudden cardiac death (I was actually pronounced dead), and several other medical issues. So I decided to chronicle some important phases in my life so that relatives, friends and anyone else who might be interested can read this and know that I was here once.

All details are as true as I can remember. Some names have been changed to protect the innocent and the not-so-innocent.

So, let us begin.

Paul Polka, 2015

Chapter One

Pittston

On May 26th, 1937, I came into the world in Pittston Hospital, Pittston, Pennsylvania. Mom was a good-looking 22-year-old. Dad, 30 and also good-looking, was born in Italy but was brought to the US when he was about five years old. He owned a restaurant called the Pittston Diner which, as it expanded, was called the Twin Restaurant. It was by far the best restaurant in town.

Our house was situated overlooking the Susquehanna River which lay just beyond some railroad tracks separating Pittston from the more desirable West Pittston. Our house was bounded by Johnson Street on one side and a narrow alley on the other side. It was a moderately large one with a second floor containing a full kitchen, two bedrooms, living room and a small "sewing room." The unfinished basement had a coal furnace, a coal bin and a hopper to feed the furnace, which had a voracious appetite for anthracite coal. My older brother, Mickey, and I had the job of keeping the furnace supplied with coal. At one point we were both so small that we would fill a large can with coal, then put an iron pipe through the two handles and both carry it to the hopper and dump it. A "worm" revolved once a second and carried the coal into the furnace. If the worm was left uncovered, coal gas would escape, which could be dangerous. Coal was delivered in one-ton increments and was shoveled by one man down a metal chute and into the coal bin. Since the coal was delivered wet, it would freeze in the wintertime and clog the chute. The man would get a container of hot water from Mom and slosh it down the chute until it unclogged.

I'm the charming fellow in front, about age 4.

My Uncle Cy delivered milk from a horse-drawn cart. The horse knew the route. As a little boy, I thought he was very rich since he had so much change in his pockets. The milk bottles often froze in the winter, pushing up the cardboard lid. Uncle Cy also had worked in the coal mines and eventually died of black lung disease.

Our backyard was small and had a pear tree which was struck by lightning and had to be taken down. At the end of the yard was an alley which had room for one car, but I never saw a car there. The back of the house had a sidewalk that led to the alley. Alongside the sidewalk was a

With my parents for my first communion, 1945

garden which was tended to by my mother's mother. Grandma had peppers, corn, tomatoes, basil and a gorgeous red rose bush. She also had three daughters: two in Pittston and one in Wilkes-Barre. She spent several months a year with each of them and was a very religious Catholic who read from an Italian bible every day, then started at the beginning again. She was kind and gentle. Once, when she was with us, two of my Irish friends and neighbors commented on how funny her broken English was. I asked them for an example of their Italian. End of discussion. When I was a junior in high school, she died while living with us, and the viewing took place in our house. People were lined up from our living room to about thirty feet outside the house for the viewing.

My parents, Mickey and me, 1946. I'm the one scowling, as usual in pictures.

We had a large attic which contained the usual attic junk, dust-covered suitcases, lamps, fans, etc, as well as a couple of dress forms that Mom used for sewing clothing. Brother Mickey and I came up with the absolutely brilliant idea of making flaming arrows by soaking small bits of old rags with gasoline from a can of fluid we used for the engine in our model airplane. Our bow and arrow was just a toy but could shoot arrows short distances. We, of course, shot the flaming arrows at the dress forms. Nothing ever caught fire and the arrows didn't stick in the dress forms, but it was a dumb thing to do anyway. Mick should have known better; after all, he was two years older. In fact, he still is.

Mick was very good at building model airplanes that we flew at the end of a long control wire. They could only fly in circles

4

until the gas ran out but were a lot of fun. Mick only allowed me to stick decals on the planes. His fascination with aviation eventually led him to a long career in the aerospace industry,

which included working on the space shuttle engine, among other things. That all came about when, while working as a draftsman for a furnace company in Scranton, PA, he married and just upped and drove his new wife to aerospace heaven, California. Pulling a small trailer behind them, they drove cross-country to Los Angeles. When they arrived there, he had 60¢ in his pocket. Mick phoned a cousin living near LA and bummed a meal from them. He quickly found work with an aerospace company, and the rest, as they say, is history.

Mickey (right) and me, 1947

□ □ □

Back in Pittston, our gang consisted of Mickey, neighbors Joe and Franny Burns, and Bill Gafney. We played basketball twelve months a year using a basketball net nailed to a backboard nailed to a street lamp on the corner of Elizabeth Street, right in front of the Gafney house. We often also played catch with a baseball, and once in awhile the baseball would roll down a gutter and into a sewer. When that happened, we would remove a sewer manhole cover and hold Franny by his ankles while he reached down and retrieved the baseball. It was a stinky job, literally, but someone had to do it, and Fran was the smallest and lightest of all of us.

We also spent many hours down on the railroad tracks, sometimes just walking, sometimes throwing rocks into the river or at rats that gathered near a sewer outlet into the Susquehanna River. On one occasion, Fran and I were throwing rocks into the river when we spotted what we thought was a log floating some distance out near the middle of the river. The "log" was actually a dead body of a man dressed in a suit and tie. Evidently someone must have called the police because a couple of cops and others showed up with some sort of casket and with a long pole hooked the body and lifted it into the casket, which had holes for water drainage. The body was bloated and hideous. The men carried it to a pickup truck and left. We never heard or read a word about it later.

The town was known to have a fair number of Mafia residing there. Every so often, two FBI agents would come to our house to talk to my dad. They would ask him if he had heard anything in the restaurant that would be of interest to them. Dad would tell them that the men they were interested in would come into the restaurant, order food, eat the food, pay for their food and leave. Dad would always tell us that he really did not know anything, and if he did he would keep his mouth shut so as not to jeopardize himself or his family. I think that was a good way to feel and act.

With Mickey again, in back of Aunt Gert's house, 1949

We lived in the section of town called Oregon. Why Oregon? I don't know, but it's still called Oregon. The Catholic church in Oregon was named St. Rocco. Most of the parishioners were Italian. The Irish attended the church called St. John's, which was more in town, just off Main Street. My high school, Pittston High, was at the top of William Street, and St. John's was at the bottom of William Street. It made for an intense rivalry in football. My neighbor and friend, Joe Burns, was Irish and

Pittston High School,
which no longer exists,
through no fault of my own

attended St. John's where he was a star athlete in football, basketball and track. When the traditional Thanksgiving Day football game rolled around in 1951, I was a benchwarmer for that game. I tried to tell the football coach, Cy Gallagher, that our defense should play Joe very loose. I mentioned that I had played against Joe in many pick-up football games around home, and that he had deceptive speed and could blow the defense away with a sudden burst. Of course Cy paid no attention to a guy who seldom even got in a game. Our defense played him tight, and he burned us for two touchdown passes.

Then and Now

Pittston was a thriving, medium-sized town with a busy downtown. There were many privately owned businesses plus several chain stores and two movie theaters. It was also in the heart of northeastern Pennsylvania's coal country. During the end of the 19th and the early 20th centuries, the coal mines drew many immigrants from Ireland, Italy, Poland, Wales and other European countries. The work was hard, the hours long, the pay low, and the "company stores" ever present. Although there were many nationalities represented, the breakdown probably could be categorized as 40% Irish, 40% Italian and all the others, 20%.

The tunneling of the coal miners created occasional cave-ins. On one occasion, while sitting in a high school classroom, we heard what sounded like a gunshot. The ceiling suddenly cracked in all directions. We were ordered to evacuate. As we poured out to the nearest street, I saw a policeman straddling a fissure opening up between his legs. Then everything quieted down, and school was dismissed. During repairs, we had half-day classes at a middle school about a mile away. At home, too, once in a while, we could hear miners yelling things followed by a dull thud of a dynamite blast which sometimes caused dishes in our cabinets to rattle. It was illegal to mine for coal so close to the Susquehanna River, but they did so until it caused a tragic accident.

Known as the Knox Mine disaster, it happened on a Sunday. The river broke through a tunnel and flooded the mines, killing twelve miners and spelling the end of coal mining in the area. The father of our neighbor and playmate was a mine supervisor who, for some reason, decided to check on something in the mine that day. He was one of the twelve miners whose bodies were never recovered. The family had to wait seven years before the father could be legally declared dead. Soon after the tragedy happened, I walked about a half-mile along the railroad tracks to the place where the river broke through. Railroad boxcars were being picked up by a huge crane and dropped into the river in an attempt to plug up the large hole through which the river water was gushing. The boxcars would just swirl around the opening and then be sucked into the gaping hole and disappear. That went on for a while, then the idea was abandoned, and huge pumps were brought in. The enormous amount of water coming out of the mines was coal-black in color. The area mines remained closed and were replaced by a considerable number of jobs in the women's garment industry. The mine operators were never indicted for gross negligence nor assessed any fines for disregarding safety regulations.

Now Pittston is a dead town, abandoned by droves of young people who attended college and never returned, or found employment elsewhere and settled there. A few years ago, my two brothers and I were camping near Wilkes-Barre and decided to go to Pittston for lunch. When we arrived at the restaurant, which was located on Main Street in the middle of town, I got out of the car, looked up and down the sidewalk for about two blocks and only saw one person. When I was growing up there, it was hard to even walk through the heart of town due to the crowds of people. There were two movie theaters: the Roman and the American. On Friday and Saturday nights, there often was a line of people waiting to get into my father's restaurant. Once in a while, his dishwasher would not show up, and he would call home and tell me and my brother Mickey to go and wash dishes there. For eight hours of work in the busy, hot kitchen, we were each paid five dollars.

Once, during my junior year in high school when my older brother was in college, I was filling in for the absent regular dishwasher. Janet, one of the waitresses, asked me to help her with something in the basement storage area. Once there, she grabbed me and started kissing me. Just then a cook, who must have known what she was up to, shouted, "Janet, is that the help you needed?" She stopped and went back upstairs. I was very embarrassed. Excited, but definitely embarrassed.

The basement also was where an elderly lady named Mrs. Bartlett baked all the pies. Her pies were legendary and sold out every day. She was a great baker, but even more cantankerous than my dad, the owner. He could only address her as "Mrs. Bartlett," and on more than one occasion she chased him back upstairs when he started to bother her.

My cousin "Red," who was one of the cooks, was smitten with a waitress named Irene. At the time, there was a hit tune called "Good Night, Irene," and Red would continually feed coins into the restaurant jukebox to play that song. Dad got so mad, he pulled the plug and later had that record taken out. By the way, Red later married Irene.

When I was in 10th grade, I knew the center on the basketball team, Tom Sutter. I told him that if he ever scored twenty points that I would buy him dinner at my father's restaurant. Twenty points was quite a lot since the whole team usually scored about forty points. On one occasion he finally scored twenty points, and I took him to the restaurant where he ordered a decent dinner and so did I. Dad was working the cash register. I presented the check and paid the bill. Tom was amazed because he thought I picked Dad's restaurant because I wouldn't have to pay for the meals. He didn't know my father.

There was a restaurant in town almost directly across the street from my father's restaurant, called the Majestic. It was a great place for a quick meal and specialized in a chili dog with their homemade chili sauce. The thing that was unusual about it was when you were finished eating, you just walked up to the cash register and told the cashier what you had. He would add it up and tell you what you owed. They never issued you a check.

Another very popular place for the high school kids was the "Corner Shop." It was a small place that sold pizza, soda, ice cream and had a pinball machine. The pinball machine took nickels, and if you were good enough at it, it paid off in anywhere from five to fifty nickels. My friend Buddy "Ack" was expert at it. We would give him money to play the machine and often get our money back with a little interest. At school, we had a small store in the basement. Buddy would go downstairs and get you something from the store if you bought him something, too. He later became a dealer in a Vegas casino (surprise, surprise). Pizza was 10¢ a slice, cokes were a dime. Since a movie cost 50¢ a ticket, a typical date with my girlfriend cost me under $2.

The Band

My mother loved accordion music. When I was about 12, she decided that she wanted me to play the accordion. I had little interest and no desire to learn to play the instrument, but my father brought me to Deluca's music store in Wilkes-Barre to look over several models, mostly Italian- or German-made. Of course I knew nothing about accordions, so I just pointed at an 80 bass, a relatively small instrument, and my father bought it. The store owner, Jimmy Deluca, came to our house once a week to give me one-hour lessons and charged my mother $5. He would listen to me play the previous week's lesson while handwriting a new song or songs for the next week's lesson.

My older brother, Mickey, took piano lessons in Wilkes-Barre and we already had a piano in the house for him to practice on. My mother gave me her small "sewing room" in which to practice my accordion. After a while, I got to be reasonably good on the instrument and was asked to play at several parties in the homes of classmates.

While I was a junior in high school, one of my classmates, Josie Saito, mentioned to me that her Uncle Tommy had a band, and his accordion player was being drafted by the Army and would leave the band in a few weeks. From the playing I had done at parties, Josie knew that I played the accordion and asked if she could give him my name. I wasn't sure that I was capable of being in a band, but I told her she could give him my name. A few days later, Tommy Freas called and told me that if I was interested, he would like to audition me for his band, Tommy Clem Freas and The Melody Ranch Boys. I told him that I had never been in a band before, but I would audition for him. He told me to go to his candy store on South Main Street. The store was close to the grade school where I went for 5th and 6th grades, and I had frequently gone into his store for some candy.

My smiling visage at age 12, about 1949

On the appointed day, I lugged my heavy accordion about a half-mile to his store. He greeted me warmly and said he sometimes ate in my father's restaurant. Then we went into a back storage room where he introduced me to a guitarist named Burt Orlando. Both Tommy and Burt were in their 30's, which to me seemed old. Tommy picked up his guitar and asked me to play a polka. I played the "Guitar Polka," which was one of about only three that I knew. After asking me what the key was, he started playing with me. When it ended, Tommy asked me if I knew any country-western songs.

"No."

"Can you fake it?"

"No."

"Do you know 'chord families'?"

"No."

Things were going just great. I couldn't wait to get out of there.

I still remember that he told me that in the easiest key, C, the chord family was C, F, G, then F for the chorus, then usually a D. He told Burt that he, Tommy, was going to sing "Mansion on the Hill." They played and sang the song, then told me to accompany them. I found that, much to my relief, I could sense when the chord was going to change, including the D chord in the verse. Of course I stumbled, but we continued on. He said we were going to play "Your Cheatin' Heart," a classic Hank Williams song that was popular in the '50s. I played, but did not do well with it. Tommy then told me that the coming Friday night, the band was going to play at a bar/restaurant in Scranton called The Savoy. His current accordionist, Steve Swetson, would be there, and he wanted me to sit and listen to him and get the feel of what they did.

The place was smoky and loud. Steve told me that all that was in my favor, since the music was secondary to the drinking and eating. I could tell that he was right. I noticed that the band had absolutely no sheet music with them. Steve said that neither Tommy nor Burt could read music. When I observed that Tommy would allow anyone to "guest sing" just by asking, Steve said that could be a challenge since often the singer would change keys abruptly. I confided in Steve that I did not think I could fit in with this band, but I continued to practice with them, learning their repertoire of songs, and started to feel more comfortable with them. Luckily, country-western music tends to be simple in structure and leaves a lot of room for interpretation. Back in the 1950's, there was a trio named The Three Suns. I really liked the accordion player's style and started to copy it. I copied it so much that I began to play like him, albeit with far less talent. I can't really explain it, except to say it involves playing a lot of extra notes on the way to the main ones. Clear as mud, isn't it? I told you it was hard to explain. It became so natural for me that I still play that way on my Yamaha electronic keyboard in my home office.

Somehow, I was hired. For the band, I needed a better instrument, and my father bought a larger 120 bass accordion for me.

Tommy Clem Freas and The Melody Ranch Boys played every Friday and Saturday night at Lou's Blue Room on Main Street in Old Forge, PA. That went on for about two years. We also played other nights whenever Tommy Clem got us a gig. There was the Rendezvous, a bar on Main Street in Pittston, the Wyoming Hotel in Wyoming (Wyoming, PA, that is), and the Melody Lounge in Wilkes-Barre, PA. Whenever I washed dishes at Dad's restaurant, I received $5 for eight hours' work in a hot kitchen. My pay with the band was $14 for three hours' work and breaks. At Lou's Blue Room, I not only got paid $14, I also got much soda and pizza from the nice older lady in the kitchen, who sort of adopted me. It was amazing how much soda and pizza a teenage boy could consume.

Things were going well for me. I was listening to late night radio stations who specialized in country-western music, and I learned a lot of songs just by listening to Webb Pierce, Eddy Arnold, Ernest Tubbs, Earl Scruggs, Hank Williams, and Little Jimmy Dickens. My favorite radio station was WWVA Wheeling, West Virginia with DJ Lee Moore. I really didn't, and still don't, like country-western music. My preference is for classical (especially baroque) and jazz (especially piano and Latin jazz). I really enjoyed Dave Brubeck, Oscar Peterson, Stan Kenton, Django Rhinehart and others. There was a place in Chicago called The Palmer House where they featured jazz bands. Later on, when I was in the Air Force, whenever I had some extra money, I would take a train from Rantoul to Chicago just to hear whoever was playing there at the time.

□ □ □

Back at the ranch, Tommy Clem got us a spot on a telethon in Wilkes-Barre for some charity. I don't remember exactly where, but it was a shrine or temple. We waited in the wings for a long time, then finally got introduced. We played our theme song, "Oh, Dem Golden Slippers," followed by "Mansion On The Hill."

I guess it went all right because that's all I remember from that night.

Playing at Lou's Blue Room in Old Forge involved a couple of incidents you might find interesting.

While working there one night, as I scanned the crowd while playing, I noticed that off to my left there was a sailor in uniform with his back to me, and his girlfriend facing toward me. Every time I looked, she was looking at me and smiling. At break time I often walked directly across the street to a diner for a cup of coffee. As I passed by the sailor and the girl, the sailor grabbed my left arm, pulled me across their table and started punching me. The girl screamed. Lou, the owner, broke up the fight, grabbed the sailor and shoved him roughly toward the side door leading to the parking lot, and right out the screen door. The girl left by another door. I made the motions of brushing my clothes off and yelled, "Let that be a lesson to you!" The crowd gave me a sarcastic cheer.

Another time, a man approached the bandstand. He looked somewhat familiar, but I could not place him. He quietly called me by name and began telling me something about how a guy needs to have a little fun sometimes and how he would appreciate it if I did not mention it to anyone. I think he might have been some relative who was stepping out on his wife. I assured him that I didn't see anything. He was greatly relieved, whoever the heck he was.

Another night at the same place, we packed up and went out to the car. It was about 1 AM and we were tired. We discovered that Tommy Clem's car had four flat tires (probably the work of the mad sailor). Burt went back inside and after a short time came out with a drunk woman and her daughter, who told us that they would drive us back to Pittston. We piled into their bright yellow convertible with the top down. Tommy sat up front with the mother; Burt, me and the daughter climbed in the back. The daughter introduced herself as Ayanna. The tight quarters suited her just fine as she was all over me. Burt was thoroughly enjoying the scene. So there we were, five loud people driving too fast down the road, radio blasting, at 1 AM in an open convertible. What a sight that must have been.

The Band Hits the Airwaves

Tommy somehow got us a show on a radio station, WPTS in Pittston. It was a small station in downtown, about two blocks from my father's restaurant. We had the show for almost two years. We were on the air during the rather strange hours from 11:05 AM to 11:45 AM every Saturday. Each show began with Tommy ringing a darn cow bell and the announcer, "Strawberry Joe," saying, "And now, coming to you from high atop the Newrose Building in downtown Pittston, it's Tommy Clem Freas and his Melody Ranch Boys!!" All this while we played our theme song, "Oh, Dem Golden Slippers." We never knew what else we were going to play until Tommy said it over the air. It was the same way when we played at various places. Tommy would banter with the audience, then mention the title of our next song, and we would play it.

The studio was small and had a visible control room with Strawberry Joe behind the glass. He also did time checks, weather, announcements and an ad every now and then. I was "Smokey" and Burt was "Spurs." Just about every week, we had a guest singer, usually a girl in a cowgirl outfit. I never understood why they dressed that way; it was radio, not television. When asked what key they were going to sing in, they often didn't know. We would have them sing a little of the song until one of us, usually Burt, would call out the key. Then I would ask the girl to sing the last line, which then became the intro.

We did not receive a nickel for the radio shows. Tommy Clem would use them to mention where we would be appearing during the next week. Yes, we actually had people who, after catching our radio show, would come to hear us.

Whenever my mother drove me to the radio studio, she would sit on one of the metal folding chairs for the duration of the show. On one occasion, after a song ended, she clapped, and I had to motion to her not to do that. You have no idea how loud just one person clapping can be.

I haven't really told you much about Tommy Clem. He had a raspy voice, the result of drinking too much raw alcohol when he was in the Army. He also had a problem of some sort with his left foot. When he walked, he couldn't put his left heel down and walked only using his toes on the left leg, but not his heel. Tommy also did all the talking on jobs and on the radio. He would banter easily with the crowd, get their attention, then play and sing. Even with his raspy voice, Tommy sounded good. Burt never sang solo but did harmonize on some numbers. I always kept my mouth shut. Odd, but I've been told to do that many times in my life.

Cutting Our First – and Only – Demo

Tommy set up a demo recording at a studio in Scranton named Largo Records. The song we were to record was called, "I

Lost My Lover in Korea." Written and sung by Tommy. Hmmm, how to describe the song.... Dumb. Yeah, that's the right description: dumb. It was simple and repetitious. Burt and I did not want to record it, but Tommy prevailed. The first two efforts didn't satisfy us or the studio manager, but the third try was accepted – I don't know why. Of course nothing came of it. Tommy was given the demo, and it was never spoken of again. RIP. Amen.

Chapter Two

School

I do not remember much about my early school days (grades 1 thru 4), except that the school was only about two blocks from home and no longer exists. However, I do still remember first or second grade where I was very taken with the pussy willows that the teacher had on a windowsill. My first-grade teacher was Miss Howelly (who was also my mother's first-grade teacher). Each day she gave us a short handwritten list of words and we were expected to be able to spell them the next day.

Yet another smiling picture. Me and my friend Lenny Bonfanti (in the hat) about 5th or 6th grade. I went to school with Lenny for 12 years.

The next school, grades 5 and 6, were at a school about six blocks from home. It was there that I learned how to handle bullies. A kid named Sammy enjoyed poking other kids in the stomach and pushing them into the wall. When he tried to do it to me for the second time, I punched him in the face. Blood started to flow out of his nose, and he howled in pain. Even though he was bigger than I and could beat me in a fight, he decided to just pick on prey who wouldn't hurt him.

Grades 7 and 8 were in the far end of the high school. We had a math teacher named Miss McDonough, who we called Mickey Donuts. We thought the name was hilarious.

At the close of 8th grade, there actually was a graduation exercise. It was supposed to commemorate moving into high school. It also started a long-standing bad relationship with my father when I had my diploma show my name as Paul CHARLES Polka. My middle name was really James, after my father, so this was intended to be a slap at him. I didn't think he would even notice it, but he sure did. Although he never mentioned it to me, Mom told me how angry he became when he saw my name on the program. She told me I should not have done that. I still have that 8th grade graduation diploma, and it wasn't the last time I did that.

My 8th grade diploma, in the name of Paul Charles Polka

Ninth Grade

Ninth grade was uneventful except for the several times Mom was called to the school to hear complaints about my behavior, such as disrupting class, clowning around, not doing homework, etc., etc., etc. It was dawning on my parents that I was not a good student. The problem with that was that they thought it was lack of intelligence when it was actually lack of maturity. I did virtually no homework, no studying, yet my grades were decent enough. On the other hand, my older brother Mickey had great grades, was no problem for teachers, and was more obedient and compliant at home, all in stark contrast to my behavior. That essentially made my school and home behavior look even worse than it really was.

"Wow, what a fascinating record!" Actually, I was just posing with a friend for a yearbook picture.

At the beginning of each high school grade, when teachers saw my name, they invariably smiled and appeared happy to know that I was Mick's brother. They expected the same comportment from me. That usually changed quickly, and with good reason.

Tenth Grade

In 10th grade, I met another student, Carmen. We were kindred spirits and had loads of fun both in and out of school. He was the funniest and most quick-witted person I knew in school. We did improvisational comedy skits for our classmates. We also wrote "The Say of the Day" on our homeroom blackboard, and other students would peek at the blackboard for the latest "saying."

One incident I still remember is when we went to a movie together that featured a Texas oilman, complete with the Texas drawl. After departing the theater, we continued to parody the oil man until I became weary of doing it. However, Carmen continued on and on and on. I could not get him to stop. Finally, while walking down Main Street, I slapped his face hard. He just shook his head and returned to normal speech. But a lady saw what I did and berated me for slapping my friend.

In Miss Long's geometry class, Carmen and I sat across the aisle from each other. Miss Long was in the habit of having the students grade each other's tests. Then, when she called out a student's name, the person who scored his/her test would call out the score. You can probably figure out what we normally did. When she would call out Carmen's name, I would say 85 or 90 or some such score. When she called out my name, Carmen would stand up, clear his throat dramatically and say, "It is my honor and pleasure to report that, yet again, my friend Paul has scored 100 percent!"

We had the kind of desks that you could raise the lid of and put books or other things in them. Secretly, using white chalk, I opened the lid of my desk and wrote $2 + 2 = 4$, $2 + 3 = 5$ and so on. During a geometry test, I furtively opened the desk lid, took a quick look and closed the lid. Miss Long slowly walked to my desk, reached down, opened the lid, saw what I had written, and just turned around and returned to her desk without a word.

Miss Long was a good soul and good-natured. I'm certain that her overall good nature came in handy with two clowns like me and Carmen to deal with.

The Bottlecap Caper

One time, Carmen and I heard about some charity drive that involved collecting used soda bottles. We decided to have a fake "charity" for Miss Long. We spread the word among the underclassmen that we wanted to do something for her. We said that if we collected enough bottle caps, she might win a cruise to Cuba. Mostly freshmen and sophomores got together and collected hundreds and hundreds of soda bottle caps, put them in two large sacks and triumphantly brought them into her classroom. Sadly, Carmen and I were not present when the sacks were given to her, but we heard she was speechless. The following Monday, Carmen and I (who else?) were in Principal Frank Early's office. He told us that he was thinking of moving his office to right next door to Miss Long's homeroom to spare us the long walk to where his office was actually located.

Mr. President ....Not

Regina "Ma" Murphy was the Latin teacher. She headed the Latin Club, for which to be a member you had to have at least an A average in Latin. It was easily my worst subject, and I never got above a B in it. An election was being held to determine the president of the club. Unfortunately, she opened the voting to all Latin students. My slightly deranged classmates got together and I won the presidency by a small margin. "Ma" Murphy was outraged, OUTRAGED at the travesty. After a scathing scolding, a new president was announced.

By the way, my brother Mickey was president of the Latin Club two years before my "victory." The only difference was, he was actually in the Latin Club and won his election fair and square.

Other Oddities

My chemistry and physics teachers were sisters, Katherine and Esther McHale. Katherine had a wooden leg; Esther had a habit of snapping pencils in half during class. There was also a kid named Rizzo, who once or twice a week would just walk into the teachers' closet and scream. Then he would calmly come out and sit at his desk. No one ever commented on this.

My Football Career

I tried out for the football team as a sophomore but did not make the cut. I tried again in my junior year and made the cut but didn't get in any game. In my senior year, I made the cut and played enough to earn a letter, which I still have in the original stapled plastic pouch. Two somewhat noteworthy things happened that senior football season.

We were getting ready to play Old Forge, a powerhouse team in the Lackawanna League. They had a quarterback named Corny (Cornelius) Salvatera, who was a running quarterback

I'm #20, in the front row next to my good friend, Carmen (#24).

before there were high school running backs. We were told that he was very slippery and strong runner. The coaches impressed upon us that we were to ignore his legs, just concentrate on his stomach because where his stomach was, he was. Otherwise, he would fake us out with his leg motion.

During the game, Corny ran wild over and through us. In the fourth quarter, Tiger Pisano, our best lineman, raised his arm going back to the huddle. That was his usual signal that he needed a rest.

(Back then, there were no offensive teams or defensive teams. If your team ground out a lengthy drive and scored a touchdown, you didn't come out; you just ran back upfield and kicked off to the other team.) Anyway, Coach Sobesky sent me in to replace Tiger. After about two running plays, Corny dropped back to pass but took off running. I followed him. He changed direction and headed right toward me. I locked in on his stomach, and gave ground, and more ground. Corny put his head down and ran full tilt toward me. When he got close, he lowered his head and hit me with his helmet, literally running over me. I did not black out from the collision, but lay groggily on the field. Somebody eventually tackled Corny down near our goal line. While I lay on the field wondering what truck hit me, the coach arrived with our water boy. Coach looked down at me and said words I still remember: "Way to go, Polka! You damn near almost slowed him down!"

Corny went on to star at the University of Pittsburgh.

Now, the other football memory. During the season, the coach named a senior as co-captain for each game regardless of whether he was a starter. Well, when my turn came around to walk out onto the field for the traditional coin toss, the weather was awful. It was very windy, cold and snowing heavily. It was a night game, and when I looked up, the stadium light poles were swaying in the wind. The crowd was very sparse and getting sparser rapidly. I walked out on the field with the real team captain, Tiger Pisano, and we approached the head ref. He showed us the gold coin and told us what was heads and what was tails before flipping the coin high in the air. I called "heads" as ordered by the coach, but the strong wind took the coin and blew it about five feet away, buried in several inches of snow. We all hunted for it and eventually found it. It was tails. Then it was announced over the PA system that the game was officially cancelled. That was my game as co-captain.

The team trooped off the field to the waiting school bus for the drive back to the school to change out of our football uniforms. We didn't have to shower, so my friend Carmen and I walked back into town to get some hot coffee and a bite to eat. The first place was already closed. The second place, the old reliable Majestic, was in the process of closing but took pity on us and served us some coffee and chili dogs, which we had to consume quickly.

Star Pupils

During my high school days, there was no internet. To compile data for a school paper, it was usually necessary to visit a library. For our senior English class assignment, I chose the topic "Uses of Radar During World War II." My good friend Carmen wasn't interested in doing any research, but we boarded a bus to the Osterhout Library in Wilkes-Barre, where I went through the tedious process of leafing through the card catalogs and found several sources of pertinent information. Carmen spent the time trying to pick up girls. My quest was more productive than his.

I wrote my paper based on my reading and notes. Carmen decided that he would wing it. He settled on a title something like "Little-Known Inventors and Their Inventions." He made the whole thing up. The so-called "inventions" were things like pneumatic door closers, swizzle sticks, self-winding wristwatches and a few other things along with the fake names of their inventors. It must have gone on for at least three or four pages, and it was all a total fabrication. I received a B for my effort. He got a B+.

That experience was to spawn a similar one for me twenty years later at Immaculata University because of an unaccountable dearth of information on the subject of "The Assimilation Of Dutch Immigrant Children Into American Society." A Pittston up-bringing can come in handy now and then.

Damsels in Distress

One day Carmen and I came across two young girls looking under the hood of their car. Of course we sprang into action to help them. They said the car engine suddenly died on them.

Carmen told me to get in their car and slowly open and close the driver's door. Not even questioning that rather unusual approach, I got in and slowly opened and closed the door while he fiddled around under the hood. Then he told me to slam the door hard and turn on the ignition. I did that, and the engine started right up after a couple of coughs. The girls were amazed. So was I. Of course, so was Carmen, but he shrugged it off with, "Strange how some things just happen."

Eleventh and Twelfth Grades, and Beyond

My junior and senior years were a total blast. I had two steady girlfriends, was on the football team and was hired by a band and earned more money than I needed at the time. However, things at home got worse. My relationship with Dad reached the point where I had to avoid him whenever possible. One of the contributing factors was that in previous years whenever his dishwasher didn't show up, he would call home and tell me to go to the restaurant and wash dishes. Now, because of the band, I was busy every Friday and Saturday night, and usually had dates at least two other nights. So, when he called about dishwashing, I usually had to say no. That went over like the proverbial lead balloon. On one occasion, when I had to say no because of working with the band, he said that was the band's problem. I then made the bad mistake of introducing some logic into the discussion.

I said, "If you have a dishwasher and the band doesn't have an accordionist, that would be the band's problem. But if the band has an accordionist and you have no dishwasher, that's your problem."

He started yelling, and I hung up. I could have handled that situation better, but I didn't.

□ □ □

During my senior year, the University of Scranton, which at that time was a men's college, came to Pittston High School to administer tests to all the boys in the class. There were about sixty of us. They said that the top 10% would be invited to take tests at the university to determine the recipients of partial and full scholarships. I was one of six boys who qualified to take the scholarship test. Interestingly, of the six who qualified, three of us

Lettermen's Club, 1954. I'm the good-looking one in the front row, fifth from the right. That's Carmen in the center next to me, surprise, surprise.

were not among the favorites of the teachers. Up to that point, neither Mom nor Dad had ever spoken a word to me about college. I don't think money was the issue because Mickey was not living at home, had a job and was out on his own. I don't think Mom thought I was smart enough, and Dad certainly wasn't about to invest a nickel for my college since I obviously was too dumb. When the time arrived to go to Scranton to take the tests for possible scholarships, I decided to not go. Neither parent ever knew about any of it. Of the five who did take the tests, two received partial scholarships and one received a full ride.

Finally, the time for high school graduation arrived in May, 1954. Both parents attended the ceremony. I remember very little about the program, except watching my three friends who received University of Scranton scholarships be honored.

The program handouts for the audience (which I still have) showed my name as Paul CHARLES Polka. Once again I avoided using James as my middle name. That was not a good idea. Dad, according to what Mom told me, was incensed, muttered a colorful variety of curses, and demanded that they both walk out. Mom would not do that, so Dad left, and Mom walked home.

Mom set up a very nice graduation party for me in our back yard following the graduation ceremony. A large number of classmates showed up throughout the evening. There was a variety of food, beverages and sweets. Everyone seemed to really enjoy themselves. After a while, Dad came up to me and started to

High school diploma, 1954,
again showing my name as Paul Charles Polka

tell me how much he enjoyed the speech "that young boy gave." At first I did not know who he meant. Then it came to me. I told him that was our class president and that it was traditional that the class president give a valedictory speech at graduation.

Then Dad moved close to me and said, "I wish HE was my son instead of YOU!!"

I should have just walked away, but no, instead I answered, "Me, too."

I really feel that was the start of him deciding to make my life miserable from then on. He was quite good at it, too.

POLKA, PAUL JAMES
Academic   *"Pokey"*

James and Sally Territa Polka.

" 'Pokey's' personality is so
   rare;
No other with it can compare."

My yearbook entry, 1954. Nobody called me "Pokey."

□ □ □

Shortly after graduation, I began searching for a job along with a lot of other recently graduated kids from the two high schools in our town. Many were just waiting to begin college. I did not have a car or even a driver license, and as one day morphed into the next, I continued to have no success in finding work. It was a disheartening time for me. At home Dad and I often quarreled over just about anything. He said I was dumb and lazy, and who would want to hire me? I realized that he was trying to get to me and make me pay for the aggravation I caused him over the years. It was working.

A very pivotal thing happened after another couple of weeks had elapsed. It was a very hot summer day and I had been doing my thing of canvassing businesses in search of employment. I was tired, hot and discouraged. I decided to walk home and get a soda and get off my feet for a bit. As I entered our house from the alley and went into the kitchen, I opened the refrigerator door and grabbed a coke. I heard a voice. It was Dad. He was on the couch in the living room, next to the kitchen. The conversation went thusly:

"Where were YOU?"

"Downtown."

"Downtown?"

"I was looking for a job."

"Looking for a job? I don't want you to look for a job!! Hide behind your mother's apron strings!!"

At that point, I just put the soda back in the refrigerator and left, slamming the screen door harder than I meant to. I could hear some loud cursing as I walked back toward the alley. I knew that I had to get out of the house but didn't know how. I did not have a job or enough money to rent an apartment, and I felt trapped. It was at that very moment that I decided to enlist in the Air Force. There was still the Korean War at the time, but there were truce talks going on at a place called Panmunjon on the 38th parallel which separated North Korea from South Korea. There was still a draft at the time, and I figured that I would serve in the military, one way or another.

I called my friend, Carmen, and asked him to enlist with me. He flatly refused but said he would accompany me to the recruiting center. A short time later, he met me downtown and we went to the Air Force Recruiting Center on Water Street.

Upon entering, we were greeted by a staff sergeant who said he would answer any questions we might have. Both my friend and I asked a few perfunctory questions, but I was the only one who agreed to enlist. I signed a few papers and was told to wait until he phoned me with further instructions. I felt relieved that I finally had a plan of action. I did not know there was going to be a problem coming my way.

Soon thereafter, the recruiter called and told me that since I was only 17 years old (barely), I would have to have both my parents' signatures before I could officially enlist. I figured that would not be a problem. I knew Mom would sign, and Dad would be so glad to get rid of me that he would sign immediately. I was only half right. Mom did sign right away, but Dad said an emphatic, "NO!!!" That confused me. I thought the enlistment would allow him to get rid of me, and me to get rid of him. BINGO!! That was it. He did not want me to escape his wrath. He wished for it to continue.

I knew that I would have to outsmart him in order to get away and figured that should not be very difficult. Dad rotated shifts at the restaurant: a week working days and then a week working nights. I simply "disappeared." If he was home, I wasn't. If he wasn't, I was. It went that way for at least three weeks. He never even saw me during that period. He probably was getting a lot of flak from Mom as well. Anyway, Dad finally relented and signed the permission papers. He claimed that he had only been concerned for my safety and welfare. That, of course, was sheer nonsense since it came from a man who drove me out of the house once and told me to find somewhere else to live twice.

I took a bus from Pittston to Wilkes-Barre to take the oath of allegiance to protect my country, blah, blah, blah. It was done. I was in the Air Force. My orders were to return to the Wilkes-Barre facility in two weeks to be transported to basic training at Sampson Air Force Base in upper New York State. I was eager to get away and sample some of life.

In the interim, Mom urged me to go around with her to visit a number of local relatives and say my goodbyes. Invariably, I would be asked how long I would be away. When I responded, "Four years," they would usually gasp, saying that was a long time. I felt that it wouldn't be long enough.

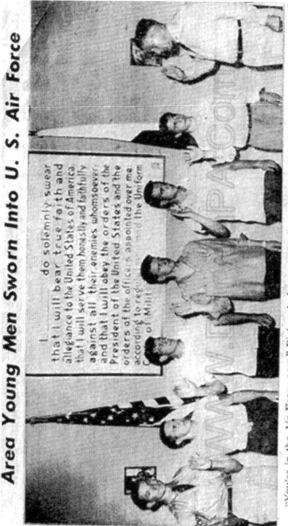

Area Young Men Sworn Into U. S. Air Force

"You're in the Air Force now." Pictured above is a group of Greater Pittston lads being sworn in the United States Air Corps at the Wilkes-Barre Veterans Administration Building during the past week.

Four of the lads are from Duryea and three of them were standout performers with the Duryea High School grid squad last season.

From left to right are: Master Sergeant Joseph Lekaunas of the Pittston Air Force Recruiting Office; John Shelly, son of Mr. and Mrs. John Shelly, 422½ Columbia Street, Duryea; Tom Shebby, son of Mr. and Mrs. Stephen Shebby, 603 Marcy Street, Duryea; Bob Yager, son of Mr. and Mrs. George Yager, 530 Green Street, Duryea; Joe Chesslock, son of Mr. and Mrs. Bernard Chesslock, 147 Pettebone Street, Duryea and Paul Polka, son of Mr. and Mrs. James Polka, (his dad is proprietor of the Pittston Diner) 8 Johnson Street, Pittston and Captain Edward J. Baker, officer who administered the pledge which can be seen in the background.

Shelly, Shebby and Chesslock were all footballers with Duryea, Shelly a back and Shebby and Chesslock were ends. All three garnered all scholastic honors.

I... do solemnly swear that I will bear true faith and allegiance to the United States of America that I will serve them honestly and faithfully against all their enemies whomsoever; and that I will obey the orders of the President of the United States and the orders of the officers appointed over me according to re... ...d the Uniform ...of Milit...

I'm the first recruit on the right.

Chapter Three

Air Force

On August 20th, 1954, my father drove me to the Air Force recruiting center in Wilkes-Barre, Pennsylvania. Not a word was spoken between us for the entire half-hour trip. As soon as I stepped out of the car, Dad immediately peeled out, probably burning a half-inch of rubber off the tires. That was my send-off.

A bus was there, waiting to transfer about thirty of us to Sampson Air Force Base in upper New York State. I boarded the bus and sat next to a guy named John, who was to become my best buddy during basic training. John and I discovered that we had played against each other in a football game between his high school, Duryea, and mine, Pittston High School. John had a girlfriend whom he intended to marry after basic training.

Upon arriving at Sampson AFB, we disembarked to the constant yelling of a drill sergeant. John said he changed his mind and wanted to go back home, but we were herded to a receiving center. There we stripped and submitted to hypodermic needles (some guys fainted) and buzz haircuts. Then came khaki uniforms which were given to us by guys who just guessed at our sizes and two pairs of heavy boots called brogans. We then marched to our barracks, which were left over from WWII. There was row upon row of bunk beds. I suggested to John that we flip a coin to see who would get the first pick. He called heads.

I said, "No, it's tails."

He pointed out that I hadn't shown him the coin, but then shook his head.

"Oh, that's right. You're from Pittston."

I chose the bottom bunk. John had a picture of his girlfriend on the shelf by his bed. He had the very annoying habit of every night loudly smacking a kiss on the picture. It was lights out at 9 PM and wake up at 6 AM, seven days a week. They tried so hard to be stereotypically military, but the Air Force just is not very military in reality. I'm glad that was the case because I am quite anti-authority by nature.

John and I wanted to go to the same place after basic training but that did not happen. I went to Illinois, and John was sent to Seattle, Washington, where he worked on B-52s. The following Easter, my Mom told me that John had come to our house looking for me in case I had gone home for Easter, but after basic training I never saw him again.

My original intent and hope was to be an Air Force fighter pilot. I was given some preliminary tests and passed them easily. All but one, that is. An office worker told me that I was colorblind, and that would rule out being a pilot or a navigator. I protested that I was not colorblind. He brought me over to a wall with a painting consisting of brightly colored circles and asked me what numbers I saw. Numbers? When I told him that I did not see any numbers, he said I was indeed colorblind. That was the first I knew of it.

□ □ □

The ten weeks of "training" was mostly boredom, followed by marching, followed by more boredom, punctuated by... boredom. I was never big on rules and regulations, which often got me in hot water.

Speaking of hot water, the one thing you really wanted to avoid was the dreaded KP. That required reporting to a mess hall at 5 AM and working until 7 PM. It was the favorite punishment meted out by the poor, demented souls called drill sergeants. John and I seemed to possess a talent for frequently annoying or enraging them. We pulled KP so often some people thought we worked there. It got to the point that when the drill sergeant started his usual, "OK, people, I need two volunteers for KP duty tomorrow morning. Now, let's see... hmmm...," John and I knew darn well that he would pick us. So we would start jumping up and down while yelling, "Pick us! Pick us, please!" Others in our unit thought we were crazy. They were not all that far off. Once, after we did our act and got our "wish," I thought John was going to cry. But we did it, and I'm certain that some of those guys have, over the years, told listeners about those crazy guys who loved KP.

Another time, we were all told to scrub the floors in our cubicles. John and I decided it would be easier to dump a lot of bleach in our buckets of water, then just use a broom to sweep the floor. The good news is that our cubicle floor looked pretty spiffy. The bad news is that we were on KP the very next morning.

One of my favorite basic training tricks had to do with those brogans (boots) mentioned earlier. The reason we were issued two pairs was because we always had to wear a freshly shined pair: one pair one day, and a different shined pair the next day. In order to enforce this critical procedure, our drill sergeant had us cut a notch in the heels of one pair. Then each day he would have us hold one foot up while he ran a finger along the heel to ensure there was a notch one day and no notch the next day. John and I decided to always wear the same pair each day while another well-shined pair was always under our bunks. So, on one day we would raise our right foot so he could feel the notch, then the next day lift up our left foot which was unnotched. He never caught on.

About halfway through basic training, we had to play what they euphemistically called War Games. It really did take place during a "dark and stormy," cold October night. Members from our unit were given red helmets, and one of the other units was given blue helmets. We were supposed to search for and capture anyone wearing a blue helmet. I spotted a blue helmet and immediately yelled, "OK, I surrender!" That was validation that I really was of Italian heritage. I was brought to a warm, dry tent for "interrogation." It seemed that others from my unit actually tried to escape being captured!! Go figure. After a while, the "war" was ended and I rejoined my outfit. Someone named Donelli was missing, and we walked and searched for him in the dark, rainy woods, calling out his name. I suddenly stumbled and fell into a foxhole onto a body, which started to wrestle with me. It was Donelli, and he had fallen asleep in the cold rain!! I suggested we have him executed but was overruled.

During basic training, we had a five-day bivouac in the woods. Prior to that, we all were given parts of tents. We were told that we either had half of a two-man tent, or a quarter of a four-man tent. I, being a city boy, figured I had half of a two-man tent. John Shelley, another great outdoorsman, said that his piece looked like mine. So we were happy to be able to bunk together out in the woods. Then we were given instructions on how to make a backpack for the five-mile hike to the encampment. It was supposed to look like a horseshoe; John's actually did, but mine did not. When it came time for the five-mile march, my brogans, instead of being tightly secured, kept kicking me in the rear end. The march itself was easy, on well-worn trails. When we arrived where we were supposed to camp and unloaded our packs, John and I put our tent pieces together all sorts of different ways, but to no avail. We each had not half of a two-man tent, but a quarter of a four-man tent. So, in effect, we had half a tent and had to sleep with our feet outside the tent. Naturally, it rained a cold October rain, so we kept our brogans on so our feet wouldn't get wet and cold. They didn't, but we had neglected to dig a trench around our tent (we thought that was just more make-work). So we spent a miserable night sleeping in half a tent in a rainstorm. We were not a couple of happy campers, pun intended.

Then came learning how to assemble an M-1 rifle. After about an hour, we had to disassemble one and then in a dark room, reassemble it. I must have done a really bad job of it because one of the instructors yelled, "Hey, Sarge, you gotta see this one!" I had four pieces left over.

Out on the firing range, we had to fire at stationary targets while in a prone position. Due to so many airmen who had come before us and the recent heavy rains, we had to lie in water that was over the small of our backs and fire about 20 rounds of ammunition. Afterward, we had to score our targets by adding up the shots in the various concentric circles and sign our names and unit number. For some strange reason, I still remember our unit number: Flight 3513. I, being from Pittston, wrote down a score that wasn't quite accurate and qualified as "Marksman." That came in handy later on, as you shall read.

Part of the training included the obstacle course. Since I was 17 years old and in fine physical condition, I did well on the course without having to fudge any of it. The one part I remember best was the "slide for life." It consisted of sliding hand over hand upside-down and backwards down a steep slope. Again, no problem. Of course, none of the training was ever used since I wound up with a cushy desk job -- darn!!

After ten weeks of learning how to keep my country safe from those who would harm it, I was told to be outside the barracks at 5 AM, fully

This was taken in June, 1955 in front of my house in Pittston

dressed and with duffle bag awaiting van transportation to the base airfield.

I saluted my good friend John, who was fast asleep, and stood outside the barracks. Shortly, a van arrived with several other guys and we left for the airport. A DC-9 from World War II was waiting for us. I sat next to a guy who told me that he had never been outside the five boroughs of New York City before basic training. The two pilots were actually the owners of the aircraft and had a contract with the government. There were no amenities, no food or drink. The ride was bumpy and very loud. We didn't care. We were done with basic training. Onward and upward!! Or something like that.

We were told that we were headed for Chanute Air Force Base, Illinois. As we circled in preparation for landing, we looked out the window and saw nothing but cornfields. My witty seatmate opined that maybe we were going to be migrant farm workers. Finally we landed and were met by a sergeant holding a clipboard. He would call out a name followed by where he was assigned. When he got to my name, he said, "3345th AIR BASE GROUP HEADQUARTERS." I asked him where that was, and he pointed at a flagpole in the distance. I hoisted my duffle bag and headed toward the flagpole. When I got close, I saw an AP, an air policeman. I asked him where Headquarters was. He just stared at me. Then I said, "Me come in peace, me not hurt you." He just pointed across the street. I was off to a great start.

I climbed about a thousand steps-- well, maybe fewer-- and opened a very heavy door. It was another world compared to the barracks at Sampson AFB. The carpet was plush, the desks polished. Everyone looked busy, yet the office was quiet. Officers were everywhere, and a few sergeants and civilian women were busily typing and paid me no attention.

A gorgeous civilian girl named Sherry approached me with, "Are you Airman Paul Polka?" When I nodded yes, she said, "Welcome, we were waiting for you." She told me that the Colonel wanted to see me. I entered the commanding officer's office. He was a large, gruff looking guy who, when I extended my hand, told me that a salute was expected from me. So I saluted. He asked me if I knew how to type.

"No."

"Would you like to go to typing school?"

"No."

He stood up. "When a colonel suggests something, consider it a command."

"In that case, I would be delighted to take a typing class."

He smiled and told me that we were going to get along just fine.

The typing class was taught by an Airman 3rd Class WAF (Women in the Air Force). The requirement for certification was typing a minimum of 35 wpm with no more than one error per two minutes of typing. Every five letters (spaces were considered letters) was considered a word. I graduated with 47 wpm and 0.6 errors per two minutes. Not great, but not bad either. That course would come in very handy for a long time.

□ □ □

Back in the office, I was told by Colonel Baker that my duties would be whatever he wanted me to do. At first, I merely familiarized myself with the inner workings of headquarters. After a few weeks, I began to realize that even though my rank was low at that point, just working there brought a number of perks. For instance, I had no KP, no marching, no inspections, no work on weekends or holidays. I was given what was called a "Class A Pass" which allowed me go off-base anytime I so desired, with no restrictions whatsoever. My room was near the main gate, just past which lay the village of Rantoul, where I often went for a bite at "Dog N Suds." The place was very much like the Majestic in Pittston.

40

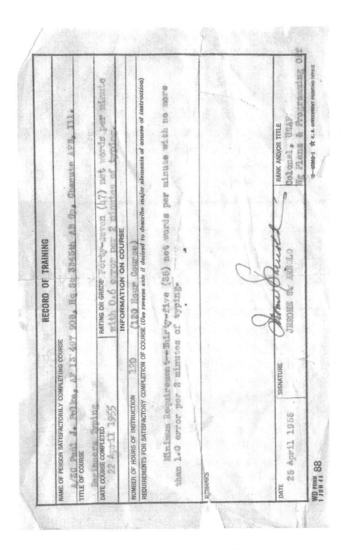

My typing school certificate

I only answered to the CO or whomever was acting in his place. The colonel had me doing everything from looking into some situation and reporting back to him, to being the Classification & Audit guy. They made the mistake of giving me access to blank certificates for all sorts of things, which allowed me to be a certified parachute rigger, jet mechanic, and meteorologist. All in all, my time there was a very good deal.

All the office military personnel were required to have on a clean, well-pressed uniform while in the office. To that end, periodically I would walk into town and drop off uniforms for cleaning and pressing. The khaki pants would come back so starched that I had to pry the inside of the legs apart so they could be worn. Back then the Air Force specified on which day to start wearing the heavy blue uniforms and which day to start wearing the khakis. So, if there was a very warm day in early August, you still had to wear the heavy blues, and if it happened to be an unusually cold early spring day, you had to shiver in your khakis. Common sense was not rampant there.

"The Kid" Goes AWOL

During the Christmas season in 1956, I went home on leave. On the return flight to Chanute AFB, our flight had to land in Dayton, Ohio due to bad weather in Chicago. The airline, TWA, put me up at a downtown hotel and told me that TWA would send a telegram to my office explaining the flight situation. My hotel room had something quite unusual: a radio that took a quarter to play thirty minutes. The airline gave me unlimited free rides to the Dayton Airport,

Christmas at home, 1954.
From left to right: me, Jimmy and Mickey

so I must have taken five or six rides there just to pass the time. Dayton was not exactly a swinging town.

After two days there, I was finally able to fly to Chicago, where I took a train to Rantoul and Chanute AFB. The next morning when I reported to the office, my civilian friend Sherry hurried over to me, pulled me to the side and told me that I was listed as AWOL. Evidently TWA did not send the message concerning the flight delay. I asked Sherry if the colonel saw the report, and she said no. I just went to my desk, found the report and tore it up. After all, I really was not AWOL.

Just another perk of working in Headquarters.

Once a Marksman, Always a Marksman

The colonel called me into his office one day and told me that I was to go to the Champaign, Illinois police firing range to re-qualify as a marksman. (My records showed I was a marksman at the conclusion of basic training.) I called Base Motor Pool and told them Colonel Baker wanted to be picked up and driven to the Champaign police firing range. I waited outside and when the Air Force blue car drove up, I asked the sergeant driver if he was there to pick up the colonel. When he said yes, I told him that the colonel couldn't make it and ordered me to go alone. The sergeant just shrugged, and I climbed in the back seat.

When we arrived at the firing range, I got out and noticed policemen firing pistols at targets moving between rocks. The targets would start and stop periodically. A man was standing on a platform watching with binoculars. I figured he was in charge and told him why I was there. He nodded and sent me over to a policeman who handed me a gun. I think it was a .45 caliber gun, but I knew next to nothing about guns. He told me to go over on the side where the targets were stationary. I fired the whole clip and only hit a target twice. He did not say a word, just watched me get into the back seat of the motor pool official car and drive away. When I got back to the office, the colonel asked how I did.

"They were amazed and speechless."

"Great," he said. "Once a marksman, always a marksman."

Batting Against the Great Johnny Padres

It was probably around 1956 when it was announced that the great left-handed pitcher for the Dodgers, Johnny Padres, was going to appear at Chanute Air Force Base and give a major league pitching exhibition. I got to stand in back of home plate behind the screen.

Padres warmed up for about 10 minutes, then started to pitch against the Chanute baseball team. From my vantage point I could identify curveballs, fastballs and every so often a slider. At that point in my life, I had never even seen a major league baseball game. The first thing I noticed was the sound of the ball hitting the catcher's mitt. The ball had to be traveling about 90 mph. Then he faced about ten players from the base team. A few of them hit some foul balls behind the plate due to swinging late. Most struck out after five or six pitches. A few batters hit weak ground balls.

Then it was announced that Padres would throw three pitches to people in attendance after a short rest. Since I was already just behind home plate, I was able to be about tenth in line.

I didn't even see the first pitch. The second and third pitches I sort of waved at. It continued like that for ten or so more batters until Padres stopped throwing. The coach of the base team said that Padres did not want to hurt his pitching arm, so he was basically just exercising out there.

The big show-off was lucky I was just getting warmed up myself.

Nice Try, Polka

All jobs had Air Force Specialty Codes (AFSC) which defined the area in which the airman was working and the skill level involved. For example, my AFSC was 73250. The 73 indicated personnel, the 2 indicated enlisted rank, and the 50 indicated skill level. The skill levels were 10, 30, 50 and 70. Our office routinely received requests for military personnel from all over the world by AFSC. If an airbase in Japan needed two people who were 64210, it meant two people in Supply, enlisted rank, at the 10 skill level.

After a while, I thought a change of scenery would be good for me, so I would peruse the incoming requests to check for 73250s. When I spotted one from a warm state or country, I would add my name to the list scheduled to go there. The colonel had to approve the list, and invariably, he would draw a red line through my name. So I decided to put my name on the list out of alphabetical order. The list came back with a red line drawn through my name and the words, "Nice try, Polka." Needless to say, I never could get away and stayed at Chanute until I was discharged.

It Ends With –arium... I Think

Our office had a "runner," someone of low rank who was used to bring forms and messages to other buildings. Our runner was a very tall young man from Texas who was not exactly an Albert Einstein. I asked him once to take something to Base Sanitation. After a long time he called me and said he was told that they did not understand what he wanted. I asked him where he was.

"The sanitarium."

"There is no sanitarium on the base," I informed him.

"Yes, there is. It's where they have a lot of pictures of planets and stars."

I finally figured it out. He was at the base planetarium.

That same guy was very tall and lanky. Once, I saw him bent over, drinking from our water fountain. There must have been some water on the floor near the fountain. He slipped, fell against the wall, tried to stand up, slipped some more, stopped moving, then tried again to stand up straight. The attempt was not successful. He fell. The whole thing seemed to take forever, even though it probably was less than a minute.

A "Martian" Visits

One time a guy came into headquarters and asked to see Colonel Baker. When I asked where he was from, he said "Mars." I stuck my head in the Colonel's office and told him that someone from Mars wanted to see him. Colonel Baker did not react to that and just motioned for me to send him in. After the visitor left, I found out that MARS stood for Military Air Radio System. Ah, we live and learn. Or at least live.

The Kotex Kid

On a more serious note, one morning I awoke with a pulsing pain at the base of my spine and some kind of smelly discharge. The smelly discharge also showed through my khaki uniform. That was definitely a no-no in headquarters, so I went to the base hospital to see a doctor. He told me to turn around and drop my pants. When I did, he immediately said I had a pilonidal cyst and to come back the next day to be admitted. I went back to the office and told Colonel Baker. He said it was ironic that a pain in the ass like me had a real pain in the ass.

The next day I went back to the hospital and was admitted and operated on. They used a local anesthetic, and the next day a nurse told me that during the operation I was doing bird imitations. The truth is I don't know one bird from another. The nurse told me that during the operation the doctor would tell me to shut up. Then a minute later I would say something like, "Now here is a yellow-bellied sapsucker." The doctor was not amused. The nurses evidently were. (Apparently anesthesia has a weird effect on me. One time, after dental surgery, my wife said that on the way to our car, I was bowing to each parking meter and saying, "Excuse me, sir.")

While convalescing in the hospital, I stopped by the rec room where there was a piano. I can't play the piano well because of not having a skilled left hand. The left hand on an accordion pushes buttons, not keys. Besides that, the buttons are not grouped in the sequence found on a piano (C, D, E, F, G, etc.). Instead, the bass is like a typewriter, with the keys grouped according to frequency of usage. So, being able to play an accordion doesn't do a thing for left-handed piano playing. Anyway, one day I stood at the piano with my left hand in my bathrobe pocket and played some things with my right hand, which was pretty darn good. A nurse stopped by and listened for a short time. She asked if I had something wrong with my left hand, and I told her it was hurt in a bad accident. She really sounded very, very sorry for me, and gave me a big hug.

I stayed in the hospital for thirty days because they would not release me until I was able to go back to my job. In a way, that was a good thing because I continued to be paid and had nothing to spend it on. When I was finally cleared to leave the hospital, it was April 1st, but there was a freak blizzard and they decided to keep me until the weather improved. The blizzard had winds so strong that snow actually was blown through some cracks around the windows leaving about ⅛ inch of snow just inside the windows.

Two days later I finally left the hospital and went back to my room. I was given Kotex napkins to wear on my rear to absorb any drainage from the operation. At the office, Sherry called me the "Kotex Kid".

In a Jam

There was a pick-up basketball league on the base. I joined a team called the Gooney Birds, aptly enough. I played as a point guard. During a practice session I went up for a rebound, and the ball came off the rim and jammed a knuckle on my little finger into the next knuckle. It didn't hurt much but looked grotesque. A teammate drove me to the base dispensary. When we walked in, there was a man behind a large oval table. I showed him my misshapen little finger. He told me to lay my hand on the table, then grabbed my little finger and gave it a quick yank. There was a loud, popping sound and my knuckles unjammed. However, it hurt really badly, and my hand swelled up. I was then given two aspirins and told to go home. The next day my hand was not hurting but was still sporting a large little finger. Since a large chunk of my job involved typing, it hampered the healing process and resulted in some rather unusual spelling on some documents. Back then, things had to be typed in triplicate using something called onionskin paper and sheets of carbon paper. When a typo happened, you had to erase each copy and usually wound up with blackened fingers from the carbon paper. Young people today would probably ask, "Why didn't you just hit 'delete'?"

Demon Rum

Since I was under 21 years of age, I could not legally drink. That normally was not a problem since I did not usually drink liquor anyway. One day, however, a friend of mine for whom I did a big favor insisted on taking me out and having a few drinks. He drove us into the village of Rantoul and went into a liquor store to buy a bottle of whiskey and some 7-Up. To this day I still remember the whiskey's name: Wild Turkey!!! We went to an adjacent field with high grass next to the railroad tracks and started swigging Wild Turkey. After a short time of imbibing what tasted like kerosene mixed with chili powder, we started to throw rocks at passing trains in between bouts of whiskey guzzling. When I started to feel sick, my friend drove me back to my room where I immediately fell asleep.

The next morning I walked on very wobbly legs to the office. I felt so sick and weak that I had to hold onto my filing cabinet when I stood up. Some people thought it was funny, I guess. Sherry started to refer to me as the "witty wino." Captain Dyer told me I needed to eat something. The mere thought of food turned my stomach, but he insisted that I go with him to the mess hall and have some coffee and food. He sat me down, went through the line and brought me some toast and a cup of black coffee. I forced down the toast and coffee and started to feel human again. Captain Dyer then told me to go back to my room and sleep. I did just that and have never been drunk since then, and that was about 57 years ago.

The Den of Iniquity

My room was really meant for two occupants and had two cots, two dressers, a table and two chairs, a window and a nice hardwood floor. At one time the building housed WAFs. My room had been occupied by the ranking WAF and had a pink bathtub. I never used the bathtub for bathing; I used the showers in the latrine. However, I did allow other airmen to use the bathtub for gambling by rolling dice up the back of the tub and letting them tumble down. I never played dice with them but collected 10% commission on the winnings of the biggest winner. It was a sweet deal for me but also for the dice gamblers since the games got protection from me because I worked in Headquarters.

Once in a while a pizza delivery man walked down hall to make a delivery and he always had extra pizzas with him. The aroma from the hot pizzas permeated the hallway and invariably led to the extra pizzas being bought. I often bought one of the extra pizzas for the gamblers. During the winters I kept a six-pack of Cokes on the outside window sill.

I only used one of the two dressers, but kept one very neat and clean in case of a surprise inspection. The other one was usually kind of messy but private.

My room was on the top (second) floor. I had a 45 rpm RCA record player in my room along with a Halicrafter radio. Early on, there were some hurricanes along the East Coast. As a result, the Air Force flew in a bunch of enormous B-52's from East Coast bases. My building was located right on the approach path of those B-52's, which shook my room to the point that my prized Halicrafter radio fell off my table.

"The Kid" Discovers Reading

Because I had no duty obligations other than my office job Monday through Friday, I had a lot of free time. I generally used my Class A pass to ride a bus to Champaign about ten miles away. There were no bus stops between the base and Champaign, where the University of Illinois was located. The bus terminal there was large and had a lunch counter. I would have a meal and then walk around town. Because of the university, there were a number of bookstores which I enjoyed going in to peruse the shelves. In high school I was not an avid reader and did not read any of the well-known classics that most kids read early on. That changed as I started to devour books such as *Huckleberry Finn, Two Years Before The Mast, Moby Dick*, etc. Then I started to delve into astronomy, which fascinated me, mathematics, and to a lesser extent, science. It got to a point where my officemates, especially my friend Sherry, started to tell me that I should take out fewer books and more girls.

A terrific woman named Hazel Moore was a civilian who was helping put her husband through the University of Illinois. His major was Animal Husbandry, which I told her sounded kind of kinky. She was huge with child and was the fastest typist I had ever seen. I called her "Dark Shadow" because of her size – I said she blocked out the sun. She liked me anyway.

Hazel kept telling me to go to OCS (Officer Candidate School), but first go to college. I told Hazel that I had no intention of making the Air Force a career, but she even wrote to ETS (Educational Testing Service) in Princeton, New Jersey, asking them to send me a schedule of the times and locations of their upcoming SATs. In a way she was quite annoying, but she had my best interest at heart. Most of the office was that way, looking out for "the kid." Being the youngest person in the office had some perks.

Problem-Solving... Creatively

A staff sergeant and his obviously-pregnant wife came into headquarters one day and seemed quite agitated. I asked if I could help them. The sergeant told me that he had been transferred to Chanute AFB from Keesler AFB, Mississippi almost three months before, but his financial record file was never received at Chanute. He said that he made many phone calls to Keesler, but they insisted the records were sent. His wife looked very tired, worried and worn out. I went into Colonel Baker's office and told him of the situation, and he told me to look into it. I told the couple that the colonel was upset about their situation and ordered me to resolve it.

It was around lunch time, and I needed time to think of something. I knew a lowly Airman 1/c would only get a brush off at Base Finance. Then while thinking about the poor, pregnant wife and her frustrated husband, an idea popped into my alleged mind. I gave my office friend, Sherry, some money and asked her if she would take the couple into town and buy them and herself lunch. Not only would that occupy them for a while, but having another woman to talk to could be very helpful to the wife. Last, but not least, it would give me time to think.

When they returned from lunch, which cost Sherry a few dollars more than I gave her, I asked them to drive me to Base

Finance. When we got there, I asked them to wait in the car and I entered what was locally known as the "funny money farm."

I was sent to three different people, with no luck. Then I went to the director's office. He was out on medical leave, but his stand-in director-wannabe actually was dismayed about the situation. Then I told him I was sent by Colonel Baker (which was sort of true), and that he requested a one-page report on the problem, the solution and the fix for what was "broken." That took place about 2 PM. I returned to the car and we went back to headquarters. The couple left for home somewhat down. I took down their number and said I would call them in the next couple of days, regardless of the outcome. At about 4 PM, a "runner" arrived with the report. Colonel Baker called me in his office.

January 1958, shortly before discharge. My room was right inside the door at top of the stairs.

"Do I want to know how you did this?"

"No."

And with that, he shooed me out of the office.

I phoned the couple with the good news. They would be paid all the back pay from the emergency fund and subsequent pay would take place on time. It felt great.

April Fool

During 1958 the Air Force started to downsize. To that end, airmen who signed a statement that they were not going to re-enlist would be allowed to be discharged up to 90 days ahead of their normal discharge date. I jumped at that opportunity. My scheduled discharge date was August 20th, 1958. I did the paperwork and had the date moved up to May 20th, 1958. My friend Sherry told me that she saw papers in the CO's office that had my discharge date as April 1st, 1958. There was no way I was going to fall for that trick. April 1st? April Fools Day!! No way!! Sherry insisted that she had nothing to do with it, and she was certain that she saw the date as April 1st.

Well, I was in a quandary. Should I pretend to fall for it, and act chagrined, or ignore it? I chose to act like I was falling for it, while all the time knowing it was a trick. Once in a while I would say something to the CO like, "Sir, how on earth are you going to run this place after April 1st without 'the Kid'?"

I would usually hear an answer like, "Oh, we'll manage somehow."

Gee, he was good. I did prepare to leave April 1st, *just in case.*

March 31st, 1958, I started to say goodbye to various office mates. There were handshakes and hugs and well-wishes, a few tears from Sherry and Hazel. I started to wonder if I really was going the next day. Either that, or they were great actors. Finally, the CO came out and said something along the lines of, "Goodbye, kid, maybe now I can get some respect around here." It was true. I was going home.

I went to Base Finance to get my "mustering out pay." It was $200, based mostly on the mileage to the original place of induction.

Chapter Four

Levittown

While I was in the Air Force, my parents moved from Pittston to Levittown, Pennsylvania. My father sold his half of the Twin Restaurant and also their home by the Susquehanna River. At the time (1955-56), Levittown was still being built in the farmlands of Bucks County and was largely unknown. The reason or reasons why they would uproot themselves from where they lived so many years is unknown. My guess is that it was connected with my father's gambling and drinking, but I really do not know.

After being discharged from the Air Force on April 1st, 1958, I decided to take a train back home instead of flying. It was the first overnight train ride in my life. I caught a train from Champaign, Illinois to Trenton, New Jersey. I booked a roomette, which consisted of a small, private room with a small bench and a window. It had a bed that pulled out of a wall, over a sink, and attached to a latch on the opposite wall over the toilet. To use the toilet or the sink at night, I had to crawl out of bed, unlatch the bed, then put the bed back into the wall.

After a good night's sleep, I enjoyed sitting by the window watching the scenery fly by. At Trenton, Mom met the train and drove to Levittown, PA. The house was a one-story rancher on a quarter-acre lot that looked bigger because it adjoined a lot belonging to the township. It was also situated at the end of a cul-de-sac. Even though the house was located in Levittown, it was built by a private builder, not Mr. Levitt. Across the street, a family named Mancia from the same area as Pittston became close friends with my parents. Also on the other side of the street were the Hoffmans, who had a young son who was a playmate for little Jimmy. I took both kids to their first circus.

My kid brother, Jimmy, was only five years old then, and we shared a bedroom with two double beds in it. After a short time I opted to sleep alone in a very small room. There I installed a cot very much like the one I had at Chanute Air Force Base and a window fan with two blades, one blowing into the room and one blowing out. It was comfortable and private. At least I didn't have a pink bathtub.

Brother Mickey was in California so I was Jim's big brother at home. We played board games together including Clue and chess, played catch with a baseball, tackle football in the backyard and basketball in a nearby elementary schoolyard. We went to Atlantic City and waded in the ocean. A few years later, I took Jimmy to his first major league baseball game. It was between the Philadelphia Phillies and the brand-new New York Mets. The Mets were coached by the legendary Casey Stengal, who had left the New York Yankees. The game was a doubleheader and it

Dad, Mom, me and Jim,
at home circa 1959

rained off and on, resulting in stopping the game and resuming it whenever the rain stopped. This all resulted in the first game of the doubleheader taking what seemed like forever to end. I suggested to Jimmy that we not stay for the second game. He said no, he wanted to see the second game, too, so I tried to drown my reluctance in loads of hot dogs, popcorn and soda.

Fortunately, there were no rain delays during the second game, and by the time we left, the excitement in Jim's voice wiped away any weariness I felt on the drive back to Levittown.

When Jim was 14, I got married and went to live in Philadelphia. As Jim entered his early 20's he began working for the railroad, and eventually he worked his way up to where he controlled all the "rolling stock" for the railroad. He currently is chief consultant for a company that builds or upgrades transportation systems and is loaned out about a week a month to a company in San Jose, California, while he lives in Tennessee and his home office is in Pennsylvania. He gets around.

The Chocolate Incident

My Aunt Mary in Wilkes-Barre made wonderful chocolate candies in her basement every Easter. Around Easter 1965, I drove up to Wilkes-Barre to pick up a load of chocolate candies to bring back to my mother, who sold it to friends and neighbors for my aunt. The candy was packed in one-pound plain white boxes, closed with a small strip of scotch tape. There were at least 20 or 30 boxes neatly stacked in the trunk of my car.

After I returned to Levittown, I went to a movie in the Levittown shopping center. It let out about 10 PM, which was when my favorite radio personality, Jean Shepard, was on radio station WOR, New York for an hour every weeknight. I was an avid listener to him in the 50's and 60's and even had an autographed copy of his book, *In God We Trust, All Others Pay Cash*. I turned on my car radio and tuned in to Shep, as we fans called him. After almost an hour, all the other cars had left, and I was alone in the dark lot. A police car pulled up, and an officer got out with a flashlight and told me to roll down my window.

'What are you doing here?"

'Listening to the radio." (A likely story.)

"Open your trunk."

That did make me a little nervous since I had a load of plain white boxes neatly stacked in there.

"What's in all those boxes?"

"Candy."

"Yeah? Where'd you get all that… 'candy'?"

"From a little old lady in Wilkes-Barre." (The story was getting better and better.)

"Mind if I open a box?" He smiled smugly, dug way down and pulled out one of the bottom boxes, yanked off the tape and opened the box. Rows of Aunt Mary's chocolate candies looked back at him.

He thrust the box back at me. "Get out of here."

Finding Work

Within a week of my discharge from the Air Force, I answered an ad for a secretary at a construction company in Levittown. They invited me in for an interview. I did not realize it was unusual for a man to be applying for a secretarial job since I had just returned from the military, where almost all the clerks were male. I don't think I was what they were expecting, and that job was not offered to me.

I then spotted a part-time job in Philadelphia as a chemical lab technician. The only chemistry I knew consisted of one class in high school and some reading I did while in the Air Force. When I went for an interview, I was led to a small lab in the back of a plant that manufactured all sorts of metal tubing. The lab had one chemist and a lab tech who was going back to college. Percy, the chemist, asked if I knew how to titrate. I said yes, though I only had a vague idea of what it was. He explained that the plant had seven or eight hot tanks for various tasks, such as cleaning, degreasing, anodizing, plating, etc. The job required going in the lab at night after the chemist went home, taking samples from all the tanks and titrating each of them. I would leave the resulting titers on his desk. When he arrived the next morning, he would calculate how many pounds of the appropriate chemicals had to be added to the tanks. It was easy and took about four hours. Of course, it took over an hour to drive each way. This was before I-95 was built and was a tedious drive, but at least it provided some spending money.

While working there, I answered an ad for a "junior chemist," whatever that was. It was at Allied Chemical, in Philadelphia, not far from my part-time job. The plant operated 24 hours a day, seven days a week. They offered me the job, but as the new guy, I was stuck with the midnight-to-8 shift. The job consisted of helping the "senior chemists" perform various tests on intermediate isomers and polymers that kept coming to the lab all night long.

In order to do both my part-time and full-time jobs, I would work the part-time job from about 7 PM to 11 PM, grab some dinner at an all-night diner, then drive to my job at Allied Chemical. That all resulted in returning home about 10 AM. Counting travel time, my workdays were 16 hours long.

St. Joseph the Worker

Mom was a churchgoing Catholic, but not a fanatic. She attended mass at St. Joseph the Worker every Sunday and some other days throughout the year. One day, during the few hours I was at home, she asked if she could ask me something.

I said, "Of course."

She then asked me, of all people, if she could receive communion at Mass even without going to confession first. I hesitated, because I knew religion is a touchy subject for most people, for some reason. Then I asked her if she thought that she might get hit by a lightning bolt if she did that.

She said, "Who knows?"

At that point, I decided to take a different tack. "Do you think that when you pray, you're talking to God?"

"Yes."

I continued, "Then why do you feel you have to talk to a mere mortal man in order to be absolved of your 'sins'? Why not go right to the top and skip the middle man?"

She smiled and admitted that she had never thought of it that way. She continued to attend Mass, but never again went to confession. I didn't get into it any deeper with her, but I felt it ridiculous that this wonderful, kind, generous woman felt it necessary to go to just a guy, who probably had his own issues, so that she could be absolved of her "sins." I strongly believe that the concept of heaven and hell is sheer lunacy. However, if they do exist, Mom is in heaven and maybe the priest is in hell. Ironic, isn't it?

Dad Goes Too Far, Terrorizes Mom

As I have mentioned, because of working and commuting about 16 hours per workday, I spent little time at home besides to sleep. On one particular occasion, after I had returned home about 10 AM, Mom seemed oddly quiet and glum. I finally asked her what was wrong. She sighed and sat down with me in the kitchen.

"It's your father."

She stopped there, and I told her to go on.

She told me that lately he was very combative with her to the point where she had to avoid him whenever possible. She said she had gone outside to pull weeds that had grown in our driveway, just to stay out of his way. He came outside, picked up a large rock in his right hand and with his left hand twisted her hair and said that he was going to smash her face. She managed to get away from him and back inside. Shortly after, while she was standing in the bathroom fixing her hair in front of the mirror, he slipped in behind her, put an arm around her neck and dragged her into the living room, threw her down on the floor and told her that he was going to get a knife and kill her. He went to the kitchen, got a knife and went back into the living room. She said that she screamed loudly, and he stopped, turned around and put the knife back in the kitchen.

I was absolutely livid at what he did. I felt then, and still do now, that even though he hated me, he knew he could not do anything physical to *me*, so he picked on her. Typical bully cowardice.

I got in my car and left for McGuire Air Force Base, where he managed a huge cafeteria. I was enraged and didn't know what I was going to do when I got to him. At the gate, I was asked for ID and to state my business. I told the guard that I had an emergency at home and needed to see my father, who ran Cafeteria 4. I gave him my driver license and proceeded. When I got to his workplace, I tried to calm myself down so as not to attract any undue attention, went in and asked to see my father, Mr. James Polka. An employee told me that he had just left to go home not feeling well.

I drove back to the gate, retrieved my driver license and took off for home. I honestly thought he could be killing my mother right at that moment.

Arriving home, I saw his car in the driveway. I jumped out of my car, and entered the breezeway, then the kitchen, no Dad. Then, in the living room Mom was on the couch under an afghan, eyes tightly clenched shut. She was shaking, *shaking!!!* on a hot, summer day. She thought I was Dad and was afraid to open her eyes.

I said, "Where is he?"

She opened her eyes and told me he was in the cellar, working on the water heater, but she begged me not to go down there because he would hurt me. That was not the scenario I had in mind.

I went outside (there was no inside way to get into the cellar), saw the open cellar door, went down the steps and into the cellar. He was standing by the water heater with a large adjustable wrench in his hand.

I walked over and yelled, "Did you go after my mother with a knife?"

He looked at me with the craziest eyes I had ever seen before or have since. He lifted the wrench above his head and said, "Yes, and I'll kill you too!"

I suddenly became *calm*, no longer shook with fierce anger, just quietly said, "Make your move first, so it'll be self-defense when I kill you." I truly believe that my apparent calmness scared him.

Then came the most disgusting performance I have ever witnessed. He changed 180 degrees. His eyes were normal, his voice almost childish when he said something about how he really admired me for standing up for my mother and that he wished he still had a mother to protect. I wanted to vomit.

I very slowly and calmly told him that I had decided not to kill him. I told him that if he so much as touched my mother again, I would file a criminal complaint with the police that he threatened to kill me and kill my mother. He would be charged with assault with a deadly weapon with intent to kill, and spend the rest of his life in prison as the girlfriend of some dirty, fat slob named Spike. It was the bastard's turn to shiver on a hot summer day.

I felt good that I hadn't resorted to violence, yet shook him to his core. He was scared. Very scared. That was another revelation for me. It reminded me of back in 5th or 6th grade when I realized that the way to stop a bully was to make it painful for him, a lesson I have never forgotten.

Dad disappeared for about four or five days. Then Mom got a call from Aunt Rose, Dad's sister in Paterson, New Jersey. She asked Mom what the story was. When Mom told her what was going on, Aunt Rose told her that she was going to tell him to get the hell out of her house.

She did, and he returned home a different person. I told him that I would go outside while he apologized to Mom, and that the apology better happen. I guess it did. Mom forgave the prick; I did not. The memory of the above still bothers me... still bothers me quite a bit.

To monitor Dad's behavior, I took advantage of the fact that I was seldom home at night. Often, I would announce that I was going out for the evening. Then I would drive down to the end of the street to a local market called Frank's Supermarket, park the car and backtrack to the house, using a small path past a bowling alley that ended at our back yard. It was summer, so for air circulation my parents almost always kept the door at the end of the breezeway open, and the television was there, too. I would creep up to the breezeway door and listen for anything like arguing or fighting or anything that was threatening to my mother. Let me say here that I never saw or heard anything to indicate that Mom was in danger or even being harassed. I also frequently asked Mom if there was anything going on that I should know about. She always said no and expressed surprise at the complete turnaround. I silently thanked Sammy, from 5th grade, for the opportunity to learn that you have to hurt the bully.

Sometime after the above episode, I might have actually saved Dad's life, unfortunately. Very early one morning, I was awakened by a knocking on my bedroom door. When I opened it, I found my father on his hands and knees, in his underwear, gasping for breath. I asked what was wrong, but he couldn't really talk. Mom was visiting upstate with Jimmy. I don't remember if there was a 911 emergency number back then (about 1960). I believe I called the police, and an ambulance and a policeman arrived shortly. A neighbor from across the street came over and helped put my father on a stretcher and into the ambulance. He was taken to a hospital and was subsequently diagnosed with having a collapsed lung. He wound up having lung surgery.

Subsequent to all this, Mom received a bill for thousands of dollars, which we didn't have. That is when I discovered that Dad had no health insurance. When I asked him about that, he explained that when he took the job at McGuire AFB, he felt the pay was not enough money to also pay for the health insurance offered by the company. So, he refused the insurance while having a wife and a small child at home. Brilliant.

I was at a loss trying to figure out how to pay the huge medical expense he had incurred, so I called my Uncle Alex in Paterson, New Jersey for advice. He told me to contact the hospital and tell them that we intended to pay the medical bill but would need terms that were manageable. I followed his advice, and we were offered a steep discount. We accepted it and eventually paid the hospital.

Dad's Demise

A few years later, sometime in November 1964, my father complained of pain in his shoulder and back. At that time, our garage had a door that had to be opened manually, and he said that he thought he hurt his back when the door came down on it. He went to see his doctor, who told him that he should go to Jefferson Hospital in Philadelphia. He was afraid to drive in Philadelphia, so I drove him there. It was determined that he had lung cancer, and the doctors scheduled surgery right away. As soon as they opened him up, however, they determined that the cancer had spread too far to be treated. He was hooked up to a machine to breathe for him through a large tube inserted through his throat. That bothered him so much that his hands had to be tied to the bed with small strips of cloth to prevent him from pulling out the hose.

My mother, who was also afraid to drive in Philadelphia, was only allowed to visit her husband for 30 minutes twice a day. We both spent the rest of the time in a lounge. Mom would not eat anything unless I brought it to her. There was a diner about a half-block down from the hospital where I would get something to eat and bring something back to her at the hospital. Sometimes she ate it; sometimes she did not.

As it got closer to Christmas and it was decided to put my father on a morphine drip, we decided it was time to call my brother Mickey and his then-wife, Regina, in California. Shortly after, they flew into Philadelphia and stayed at our house in Levittown. My kid brother Jimmy (12) was staying with relatives in New Jersey, so Mickey and Regina slept in Jimmy's bedroom. Since we all knew that Dad would die soon, I opted to sleep on the couch in the breezeway to be close to the kitchen phone when the inevitable call came.

About 1 AM, January 1st, 1965, the phone rang. I had been sleeping on the couch fully dressed, and I got to the phone before it could ring a second time. It was a doctor notifying me that my father had died. He recited some instructions for retrieving the body, and I went back on the couch satisfied that apparently nobody was aware of the call yet.

Not five minutes after I returned to the couch, the phone rang again. I figured that it was the hospital with more instructions, so I got to the phone quickly again.

A woman was on the line. She did not say hello, or her name, or my name. She just asked, "How is your father"?

I said, 'He just died."

The woman started sobbing hysterically, repeating "I knew it, I knew it, I knew it!" until I finally hung up the phone. I do not know who she was. I have always thought it very strange that her call came so soon after the hospital's call, at a little after 1 AM on New Year's Day, and she never said her name or my name.

When the others got up later, I told them that Dad had died earlier that morning. Of course there was no surprise, just relief that the whole dreadful situation and Dad's suffering was over. Mickey and I took care of the logistical aspects. Mom had decided to bury Dad's body at a cemetery in West Pittston, Pennsylvania, using the Graziano Funeral Home in Pittston.

On January 6th, 1965, Dad was buried on a very cold day. There were several inches of snow on the ground and few people in attendance. I remember that a cousin of mine gave birth to a baby girl that day. The chain of life continues on.

Mobil Oil

While my full-time job as a junior chemist at Allied was interesting and well paid, the inability to sleep during daylight hours was wearing me down. (That would be no problem these days, but it was back then.) I had to find a job during the daytime so I could sleep at night. I realized that a big part of my problem was the commute through the busy, jammed Philadelphia roads, so I turned my attention elsewhere. I heard of a brand-new research lab being built in New Jersey, outside of Pennington, a small town about 15 miles from home. The lab had the grandiose name of Central Division Research Laboratory for Mobil Oil Corporation. I was able to get an interview with them and headed for Pennington. When I arrived, I found a few hundred acres of land with a manor house, a new two-story building, a pond, and a volleyball court. I was directed to the manor house for the interview with the head scientist. I felt underdressed without an Armani suit, but the interviewer was wearing cowboy boots and had one leg up on his desk. He waved me in and offered me a stick of gum. We chatted for a short time as he told me about his son who was in some college in Florida and actually received college credit for surfboarding.

Eventually he got around to the interview. We discussed my rather skimpy work history, and he finally took his foot off the desk and ended the interview. I stopped at the front desk and asked the secretary what they did in the new building. She shrugged and said they were a bunch of very smart, somewhat wacky scientists, and she had no idea what they were doing. I liked the place immediately but figured I had no shot at the job.

The next week I was called and told to report to a Mobil Oil lab in Paulsboro, New Jersey for a physical, and if I passed it, I would be offered the job. I went, I did, and I got the job.

The job entailed supporting a scientist in his research. The one who got me as his "tech" must have pulled the short straw. He was relatively young and evidently was addicted to oranges, which he ate almost continually. The other chemists in the same group consisted of a Scot with an indecipherable accent, an Egyptian who spoke perfect English and consumed enormous quantities of coffee, and a guy who actually seemed almost normal who taught me card tricks and something called x-ray diffraction of molecular structures. Then there was my favorite, a chemist from China who, in order to concentrate, stuck small rubber stoppers in his ears. That evidently worked too well because he would forget about the rubber stoppers and not hear people talking to him. So he cut small strips of paper and pinned them to the rubber stoppers so that when he walked, they fluttered and reminded him that he had rubber stoppers in his ears. There was also one "normal" chemist who did not seem strange, but I was informed that he wrote the definitive book on Nuclear Magnetic Resonance Spectroscopy, or NMR. Today, NMR is commonly used, but this was back over 50 years ago. Oh, and there was one chemist who refused to use any of the vacuum pumps that we had on very nice metal rolling carts. He wanted a vacuum pump on a *wooden* cart, just like he'd had at Columbia University.

Gasher

I mentioned earlier that the property had a volleyball court. I was on one of our teams and during one game, a guy on the other side of the net jumped up to spike a ball hard back over the net. Unfortunately, in doing so he rammed his elbow into my head, opening up a gash near my eyebrow, which bled copiously. My friend, George, yelled for someone to get me off the court because I was bleeding so much, and it was getting slippery. The one who gashed me was named Gashay. He was, of course, henceforth called Gasher Gashay. He was also mortified at what he had done. He took me into Pennington to a doctor who gave my wound 12 stitches. The scar still shows.

We also had a basketball court for pickup games. My friend George and I would challenge any other two players to a game.

One of the chemists, Phil Landis, accepted our challenge. I do not even remember who the other player was. Phil whipped us without breaking a sweat. Then we found out that he had played for the University of Kentucky. He could have at least told us that before the match.

The Dating Pool, including the Great Penguin Débâcle of 1965

The secretaries seemed like a normal bunch, and they provided me with many date opportunities. Part of the reason was that the chemists were all older and married; I was 26 and unattached. However, even some of the secretaries had some quirks. One of them called me and asked if I would take her to the 1964 World's Fair being held in Queens, New York. She was a big ballet fan and the famous Margot Fontayn and Barishnikov were going to perform there. I agreed to take her, and we had a good time. Then I took her to the Garden State Racetrack in Cherry Hill, New Jersey. After the races, she wanted to go to a particular restaurant at the Jersey shore. We went there and since we had no reservation, waited in the bar for a table. She called out to the bartender by first name and introduced me to him. He was her husband!!! We did not date each other after that.

Another secretary had a Volkswagen Beetle, which she loved, and she constantly boasted about the gas mileage it got. Another technician and I decided to secretly add some gasoline to her car each day. Of course, she became ecstatic about the tremendous gas mileage her car kept getting. After about a month of that, we started to drain some gasoline from her car every day, and she started to complain about how much less mileage it was getting. At least the bragging stopped, so we stopped tinkering with her gas and let it return to normal gas mileage.

That same secretary, Jackie, adored penguins. She thought they were the cutest birds on the planet. She had scissors in the shape of a penguin and several pictures of them in her apartment.

On one date, I had the absolutely brilliant idea of dressing as a penguin, just for laughs. However, there was one minor problem: I didn't know how to do it. I got a couple of pieces of cardboard for wings and tried to make holes in them to somehow be able to tie them together. No luck, not even close. As the time to leave for Pennington, New Jersey drew near, I panicked and figured I would stain the cardboard pieces with black shoe polish and just hold them under my arms to surprise her when she opened her door.

I climbed the stairs to her apartment, placed the "wings" under my arms and knocked on her door. The door opened, but a strange lady appeared in front of me just as I started to quack. (I didn't know that penguins don't quack.) Then I heard Jackie's voice from upstairs asking if it was her date. Her *mother* yelled, "Oh, I hope not!"

I have hated penguins ever since.

Sometime later, Jackie met and married her automobile mechanic. Then she divorced him, then later remarried him, then divorced him again, then later remarried him. She probably would have divorced him yet again, but contracted cancer and died.

At the research lab, the cafeteria was only open for breakfast and lunch. I usually lunched with a couple of other techs and secretaries. The manager of the cafeteria was a woman who seemed to like me. During the summer of 1965, the manager's niece wanted to earn some money between her sophomore and junior years in college, so her aunt gave her a job in the cafeteria kitchen and introduced us. Joan was attractive and alluringly shy.

One day when a conference was being held at our facility, Joan was told to set up a station with Cokes for the attendees. As I walked by the display, I "stole" a Coke. (After all, I didn't have the chemistry or physics PhD that would entitle me to one.) Well, Joan was appalled at my reckless behavior and was quite annoyed with me. She still tells me about it, and it was 50 years ago.

Then once, when she was working in the cafeteria kitchen spraying some dirty dishes, I was teasing her about something.

She said, "If you say that one more time, I'm going to spray you!"

Of course I said it one more time, and she suddenly turned the spray on me and thoroughly soaked me. I took that to mean that she liked me.

On one date, she told me that she wanted to show me something neat. I was used to dates at restaurants, movies, racetracks, maybe a casino. But no, after a short drive, we pulled into a local dairy and went inside a barn-like building. There it was. It was something called a Rotolactor. It was an automated system of milking cows, with the milk routed up to a conduit which took it... somewhere. It was certainly enthralling, not to mention romantic, right? As difficult as it might be to believe, I never even knew that such a contraption existed.

Another date was interesting for a different reason. I took Joan to dinner at the Five Point Diner in Levittown. The meal was uneventful, but as we walked toward the cashier, a waitress was standing behind the counter with a chocolate cream pie in her hand. She was telling a man that if he said something or other again, she would throw the pie at him. I guess he did say it again because she hurled the pie at him. He ducked, and the pie hit me in the chest. The chocolate and the topping oozed down the front of my sweater and dripped on my shoes. I have seen that kind of scene many times but always as part of a Three Stooges movie. I am glad that Joan was my date that night because she has assured skeptics that it really did happen that way.

We always had an enjoyable time together, but I continued to date other girls from work. A couple of chemists took Joan aside and warned her that I was a womanizer. Well, I was. It was an accurate description, one that I worked -- or played -- hard at achieving.

The summer ended, and Joan returned to college in Philadelphia for her junior year. The college was an all-girls school called Holy Family College. They had strict rules concerning dress, visits and behavior. To go to the on-campus tennis court, they had to wear a raincoat until they were ready to walk onto the court. Male visitors had to be on the "approved" list. If the girls left off campus, there was a curfew.

On most weekends, Joan returned home and we usually saw each other. This was quite a departure from my usual dating activities. I dated a number of girls, and at least two drifted away after realizing that I had no interest in getting married. At the time, I was single, had a good job and pay, few expenses, lots of dates and went to five different race tracks. In short, I was living the life of the proverbial swinging bachelor. Marriage was not on my mind.

However, every now and then I would see Joan again. Then I found myself dating her more and more frequently, until it was exclusively her. Over objections and some threats from her parents, one of them being that they would not pay for her last two years of college if she continued to see me, Joan defiantly continued to go out with me. Her parents never followed through on their threats, and two years later we married, two months after she received her bachelor degree.

Joan and I were married September 2, 1967 at St. Martin's, New Hope, PA

On our way to honeymoon in Lancaster, PA

Chapter Five

Crazy Times

Within two years of our wedding, Joan and I had two children, Brian and Bridget. Both are great kids, smart, hardworking and fine people.

I obtained work as a research technician with a large pharmaceutical company. In order to have a reasonable commute to work, I drew a circle which represented a reasonable commuting distance around Radnor, PA. At the very outer edge of the circle was West Chester. I drove there and found an apartment complex called Cambridge Hall, which was situated just two blocks from the West Chester University campus. At their office, I found two men sitting at a desk drinking beer. When they saw me, they quickly hid the bottles behind the desk. They mentioned that the last building in the complex had just been completed and was situated next to some woods. I asked to see an apartment in that building and was taken to a first-floor apartment. It had new appliances, beautiful parquet floors, two bedrooms, two baths, a small kitchen and a dining room. I liked what I saw and said I wanted to show it to my wife, and if she liked it too, we would rent it.

The next day, I brought Joan. She also liked it but wanted to walk around West Chester to get a feel for where our children

*With the family in
our West Chester
apartment, circa
1970*

*Sunday dinner at my mother's house in
Levittown, circa 1970*

All piling on the bed together, 1971

With the kids, Joan and her parents,
Margaret and Jim Marion, 1971

would grow up. We noted the town was clean, orderly and friendly. It was also the county seat of Chester County and as such, boasted a grand city hall, parks, a privately owned bus company and a railroad station where you could hop a train to downtown Philadelphia. We returned to the apartment complex and rented the apartment. We stayed there for ten years.

During our stay in West Chester, the pharmaceutical company where I was a lab tech closed operation and moved out of state. Shortly thereafter, I answered an ad for a lab tech in a color-matching lab. Ever since my Air Force days, I had known I was colorblind, but I badly needed a job. Fortunately, the person who interviewed me was a chemist, so much of the interview centered on chemistry. He never asked if I could see colors, so I got the job. Often when I had to match a color, I would call my artistic wife and ask her how I could make a particular color. Sometimes I'd take my samples outside to "check them in the natural sunlight," and casually ask a co-worker what they thought of the match.

"A little too red, maybe?" they'd ask the so-called professional, me.

"Yeah, that's what I was thinking," I'd answer.

Then I'd mix a sample in the lab and give the formula to the men who would then mix a 30-gallon drum of it, used to produce thousands of yards of colored fabric to be used to make shoes, clothing, purses, furniture and more. After a short time and many color matches (somehow), the chemist owner gave me their color matching test. A bit late, don't you think? The test consisted of matching similarly colored tiles, requiring perception of very fine gradations of color. I flunked so badly that he thought that the test tiles were so old that they had faded. He had someone throw them out. After all, it could not be that your color matcher is colorblind, could it??

I matched colors without seeing them for about three years there. One day, while still working as a colorblind color-matcher, I needed to mail something and during a lunch break went to a small nearby post office. It only had one service window, and the line was long and slow-moving. While waiting for the line to move, I started to read the bulletin board. There were some tear-off sheets which read, "Need money for college? Tell us about it." They asked for just name and address, so I tore off a sheet, filled it out and mailed it right there. It was from the Pennsylvania Higher Education Assistance Agency (PHEAA). I forgot about it until a couple of weeks later I received mail from PHEAA which just asked if I was a service veteran. I checked the "Yes" box and sent it back. Once again I forgot about it. Then I received another letter from PHEAA. This one contained a check for $800. I realized that I could not earn a degree for $800, but figured I could take a few courses that could be helpful in the future.

Immaculata

Shortly thereafter, while checking mail, I saw an ad from Immaculata College (at the time a women's college, now a co-ed university). It stated that their evening division was now accepting male applicants. I called their switchboard number and told the operator that I was thinking of enrolling there. She asked me to hold while she connected me to the Evening Division director. After a short conversation, the director told me to call her secretary and make an appointment. I did so, and the next week I went to see her. She was a nun who had a PhD in economics from Harvard and taught economics during the day, then ran the Evening Division at night. We seemed to quickly hit it off, and I felt comfortable with her.

Then some very odd things started to happen.

After discussing my work background, she grew quiet and seemed to be lost in thought. I imagined that I had somehow said something wrong and started to feel quite uneasy. She then told me that she felt very strongly that I belonged there. The first thing I thought of was that she was just recruiting me since there were few men enrolled in their Evening Division. Then she floored me by saying that I would enroll there that very summer

(1974). She hesitated, then said that I would graduate in May of 1977. Three years!!! I felt that it was time to bring her back to the real world. I explained that I was married, had two small children at home, a full-time day job and only $800.

She was very serene as she explained how it would happen. First she told me I had to be a full-time student. I said that was impossible. She answered that my PHEAA grant required that I be enrolled as a full-time student (minimum 12 credits per semester) and that I would have to go to classes 12 months a year for 36 months. The grant money also required that I maintain a B average overall.

I patiently explained that the grant money could not possibly cover all that. She patiently explained, in turn, that she would talk to the financial aid officer and that I should make an appointment to see her.

Well, I made the appointment. When I arrived at the financial aid office, I was met by a stern, no-nonsense nun. She told me that the director had talked to her about me. Then she mentioned that the deadline for summer grant money from PHEAA had already passed, but Immaculata had a good relationship with PHEAA and planned to submit a request for me. She then told me to register for the first summer term. When I asked her how I was supposed to pay for the courses, she said to tell them that Sister Christi said it was OK. That's it -- just "Sister Christi said it's OK."

It was hard for someone from Pittston to believe that would work, but when I finished registering and got to the pay desk, instead of paying I said, with some trepidation, "Sister Christi said it's OK." They did not question that, and I left.

So began a tough three years of study and work. The classes ran for three hours each and classes were five nights a week. It was not unusual for me to fall asleep at the dining room table that I used as a desk after a few hours of reading and homework. Then I'd wash up and head for my job. I can recall a few times at school when I would ask somebody what day it was, then figure out what classes I had that night and head for class.

Because of my horrendous schedule, much of the housework and tending to the children fell to my wife, Joan. She did it all with few complaints and was very supportive.

Once or twice a week, after my last class, I would stop in the director's office and have a cup of coffee with her. When I would inquire about how she taught during the day and then ran the evening division until 10 PM, she would say, "Just like you do, Paul. Right foot, left foot, right foot, left foot."

Class Notes

Once, after I signed up for a physical chemistry course, I could not make it to the first class. In my absence, the rest of the class voted to change the night that class would meet. I could not accommodate the change and mentioned it to the director. She got on the phone and had the prof (who happened to be the Dean of Sciences at Villanova University) change back to the original meeting night. What a friend!!

In a history class, the prof gave each student a topic on which to write a paper. When he got to me, he asked what my major was.

"Chemistry."

He smiled. "OK. Write a paper on 20th century art."

I, of course, knew nothing about the subject, but my wife knew a great deal about it. I suppose you can guess where I got my information.

I had another interesting course taught by a commander in the Philadelphia police department. One night he brought the class down to the "round house" in Philadelphia. We went down to where hardened criminals were kept until they were transferred to a prison. He told us to not walk too close to the cells or we might get grabbed as we walked by. There were several women in our group who were continually verbally assailed by explicit sexual remarks. The room where these inmates were questioned had desks, chairs and even ash trays that were bolted down so as not to be used as weapons against the police.

Another time, that same commander was teaching our class when a woman walked into the classroom, pointed her finger at the teacher, said "Bang, bang! You're dead!" and immediately walked out of the room.

He then said, "Your favorite teacher has just been shot dead. You were all eyewitnesses to the crime. Let's see if we can get a description of the killer."

The only thing that was unanimous was that the shooter was female. The estimates of height and weight varied greatly. Two people said she looked Spanish. Some said one shot was fired, some said two, and two others said three shots were fired. The point was well made: eyewitness accounts are not necessarily accurate.

I really struggled with differential calculus taught by a very stern nun. I found it hard to find the time to dig into a difficult subject like that. While leaving a class one night, the professor stopped me and asked to have a word with me. She told me that as a chemistry major, I could not graduate without differential calculus, and it looked like I might not make it. It was about four or five weeks until graduation, so I asked if there was anything I could do. She told me that I could come to her office every Sunday for a three-hour session until the final exam. That floored me. I was already overextended, but I did as she suggested and trudged to her office every Sunday. It is difficult to explain just how long three hours can seem with just you and a calculus professor. There were no rest breaks, just three hours at a small blackboard in her office.

When final exam time arrived, I took the exam along with about six other students. After about two hours, I was the only one left in the room. When I finished, I felt unsure about how I had done but figured it would be close. It was after 10 PM when I left the building and headed for my car. Then I heard a tapping noise, turned around, and saw the prof at the window, a big smile on her face and showing two thumbs up. It was the only time I ever saw her smile. I didn't feel as tired anymore.

Graduation

The next hurdle was "comps." That consisted of standardized tests in the various college majors. Immaculata was just one of a number of schools that participated. You had to attain at least the average score of all the people taking the test in your major. I did, so I was cleared to graduate. The Evening Division director asked me to come to her office. She told me that she wanted to review my file and ensure everything was in order before graduation. She then handed me two $1 bills. I asked why she was giving that money to me. She replied that at one time Campus Security had fined me for not having an up-to-date parking sticker, and she put the money in my file and now was returning it to me. She then hugged me for an uncomfortably long time and kissed me on the cheek. I never saw her again. I was told that she left her Immaculate Heart of Mary order and returned to secular life.

Mom came to my graduation in 1977. I was the third man ever to graduate from Immaculata.

Finally, in May, 1977, I received my bachelor degree. It was exactly when she had told me it would happen. I can't explain that. I just know that she was special.

Her office, though nice, was not air-conditioned. At one point I had told her that when I graduated, I would install a window air-conditioner for her. Although she left her religious order just before I received my degree, after I was hired by the federal government I bought a small 5000 BTU conditioner and brought it to her former office. Her replacement, a man, was in there. I told him I had an air-conditioner for the office. He asked me who bought it. I told him I was just the deliveryman and offered to

With Joan, her parents, and the kids
at my graduation

install it for him. He declined and said he would do it. Too bad Sister Agnes could not enjoy it, but I had kept my promise.

One of the students graduating with me was a young girl who had become a good friend of mine. Her name was Kathy and she was an English major in the day school. One evening I went down to the basement between classes to where there was a "break room." It had various machines that vended coffee, tea, soda, chips, etc. While there, I noticed a girl laughing loudly while reading a book.

I asked her what was so funny. She ignored me, and I went back to my coffee. Moments later she burst out laughing again. I repeated my question. She looked up, saw me looking at her, then got up and plunked down beside me. She told me that she was legally deaf and needed to read lips. It turned out she had been reading H.L. Mencken when she was laughing. I told her about how I enjoyed P.G. Wodehouse. During our conversation she mentioned that she was a day student who taught a non-credit class in the evening to high school seniors who intended to attend college. The course was called Effective Study Techniques and met three nights a week. She was an interesting and thoroughly delightful conversationalist. We looked for each other on the three nights a week that she taught class. This was at a very Catholic university. I say that because she giggled and told me that one of her professors mentioned that she was seen frequently in the company of a *man*, a *MARRIED MAN!!* So I invited Kathy to our apartment to meet my wife. Joan immediately liked her also.

Confronting Ghosts

Sometime later, Kathy asked if I would take her to visit the high school from which she graduated, which was considered a "feeder school" for Immaculata University. Kathy alluded to having some very bad memories from there, and she had never been back again after leaving. I do not know what any of those bad memories were; she never explained them. She just wanted to go back to that campus and "confront the ghosts," even though she was scared to go back there. I drove her (she could not have a driver license because of her hearing disability).

When we arrived, she sat on the grass in front of the entrance to the school. I sat on a large rock about twenty feet away from her to give her some privacy and still be close if she needed me. She just stared at the building, lost in thought. A half hour later she got up, wiped away some tears and motioned she was ready to leave. I felt proud that she picked me to go with her so she could "confront the ghosts."

Kathy then enrolled at Northwestern University, near Chicago, where she earned a Ph.D. Later, she became an officer in

MENSA, met a man there and married. She has since written and published two books about English royalty.

Chapter Six

The Feds

Upon graduation, I started a search for employment more suited to my degree. While perusing the *Philadelphia Inquirer*, I noted that there was a job fair being held at the Philadelphia Convention Center. I decided to attend the fair.

Upon arriving, I was stunned at the large number of job seekers already there. At minimum, a bachelor degree was required, and the fair was being touted as an attempt to halt the "brain drain" caused by so many people leaving Pennsylvania after college. The lines were long in front of all the signs with the various employers' names on them. It was the same situation in front of the federal government sign, and as I started to move along, I noticed a sign that read "Federal Government for Mathematics and Science Majors." There were far fewer people waiting to talk to a representative. When my turn came, I sat with a man who explained that the Feds were hurting for math and science people, and those who were recruited would be placed on the "fast track," which meant rapid advancement after the initial two-year probationary period. He said I would be required to take the PACE test (Professional Administrative Career Examination), and I would need a copy of my degree in order to be administered the test.

I jumped through all the hoops and eventually took the PACE test in Philadelphia. It was long (three hours) and difficult, but I did ok, I guess. Shortly after the test, I received an invitation to be interviewed by the Naval Air Technical Services Facility (NATSF) in Philadelphia. It was situated on a military compound. Although run by civilians, it was overseen by U.S. Navy and Marine Corps officers.

When I arrived at the compound, I saw that there were about a dozen buildings. I could not get by security at the gate since I had no employee badge and was told to find parking off the compound and sign in at Building 1. After being questioned and searched there, I was told to report to Building 26. That was a bit confusing since I could not see anywhere near 26 buildings. After getting a map of the whole facility, I set out to find Building 26. To make my day complete, it started to rain. Of course I had no umbrella or raincoat to prevent my clothes and hair from getting soaked.

Finally, I arrived at Building 26, a tad wet and grumpy. As I entered the building, I found that there were two organizations inside. Naturally, I picked the wrong one to enter. A civilian asked what I wanted, then directed me upstairs to what he referred to as "the Taj Mahal." There was no elevator, so I trudged up the stairs and entered NATSF. I was met by the commanding officer's secretary. She laughed when I apologized for forgetting to dry myself after taking a shower and suggested a visit to the restroom to towel off.

After drying off with many paper towels, I went back to the secretary who brought me to a room with five men sitting behind a table. Four were civilians and one was a Navy commander. One of the civilians was a chemist, and we connected right away. All of them, except the commander, were supervisors of various parts of the facility. The interviews went well. I generally am much better at interviews than I am at actually doing the job.

The chemist invited me to have lunch with him at a nearby diner. I accepted and we talked at lunch about everything except the job. Then at the end of lunch he asked me what I thought about chemical warfare. I told him that I didn't like any kind of warfare. We briefly discussed HEU (highly enriched uranium) and drove back to the compound. The six of us reconvened, and I was asked if I felt there was anything in my past that would hinder my being granted a secret clearance. I said no, and the interview was finished. I was told that they would let me know yea or nay within two weeks.

Three weeks later I accepted their offer and officially became a fed. I was told that I would train under a woman named Marge Shire. She was a mirthless person who was a stickler for proper protocol. That was perfect for a blatant rule-breaker and rule-ignorer like me.

□ □ □

On my first official day on the job, Marge dropped an armload of papers and books on my desk. I asked if she wanted me to file them. She said no, they were regulations for the procurement of technical documentation concerning the care and feeding of airplane weaponry, test sets and personal survival of Navy and Marine fighter pilots. Then I was supposed to arrange meetings with Boeing, Grumman, McDonnell Douglas, Collins Radio, Naval Air Systems Command, various arsenals and Government Printing Offices. A lot of the material contained acronyms with which I was totally unfamiliar. Just a few examples were NARF (Naval Air Rework Facility), RFQ (Request For Quote), APML (Assistant Program Manager for Logistics), DEFCON (Defense Condition), and NPPSO (Navy Publication and Printing Service Office). It went on, page after page. I thought about just walking away and returning to my usual, comfortable, understandable laboratory environment. Then I thought of the pay, security and marvelous benefits of this job. No contest. I would tough it out.

My desk was immediately behind Marge's and if she wasn't at her desk, I had to answer her phone. Sometimes the person calling would say, "This is DefConCom, London." That would mean

Defense Contracting Command, London. At least I understood London.

After about three days, Marge said we were going to Grumman, in Bethpage, New York, to hold a meeting on the E-2C aircraft produced by Grumman. Gee, my first business trip. (By the way, Grumman Aircraft Corporation was always referred to as GAC, pronounced "Gack.") She drove us in a rental car, not a POV (privately owned vehicle). I was getting to almost understand the government lingo.

Marge ran the meeting efficiently, relentlessly covering mostly financial and delivery items. At one point, she asked me to retrieve ECP (engineering change proposal) 524 from her packet of files. I handed it to her and for the first time, heard her laugh out loud. What I thought was ECP-524 wasn't that at all. Grumman had an officer named Edward C. Pereteck. Any letter he dictated to his secretary had, in the upper right hand corner, the letters ECP followed by the number of the missive. So, it had absolutely no connection with Engineering Change Proposal 524.

After a while, Marge was promoted to GS-14 and moved into her own office. She summoned me, and told me she was giving me the E-2C, F/A-18, AV-8B and Big Eye Chemical Bomb programs to manage. I was stunned. I guess it showed from the look of utter terror on my face. She said, "Paul, you're going to be good, you're going to be very good." Quite a warm compliment coming from Miss Ice Cube.

□ □ □

It wasn't all uphill at my new job. After I settled in and became more comfortable with the demands of the work, my usual office banter came back.

Once I somehow ended up in a cooking contest with a co-worker, Rita. Naturally, I had to play it up. Here is the flyer I personally designed for the event:

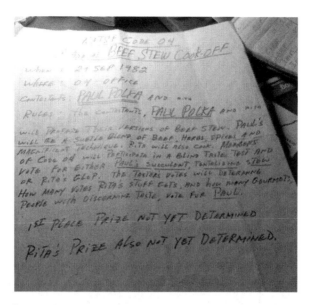

It reads:

NATSF CODE 04
1ST ANNUAL BEEF STEW COOK-OFF

WHEN: 29 SEP 1982
WHERE: 04 OFFICE
CONTESTANTS: <u>PAUL POLKA</u> AND RITA

RULES: THE CONTESTANTS, <u>PAUL POLKA</u> AND RITA WILL PREPARE THEIR VERSIONS OF BEEF STEW. PAUL'S WILL BE A SUBTLE BLEND OF BEEF, HERBS, SPICES AND MAGNIFICENT TECHNIQUE. RITA WILL ALSO COOK. MEMBERS OF CODE 04 WILL PARTICIPATE IN A BLIND TASTE TEST AND VOTE FOR EITHER <u>PAUL'S SUCCULENT, TANTALIZING STEW</u> OR RITA'S GLOP. THE TASTERS' VOTES WILL DETERMINE HOW MANY VOTES RITA'S STUFF GETS AND HOW MANY GOURMETS, PEOPLE WITH DISCERNING TASTE, VOTE FOR <u>PAUL</u>.

1ST PLACE PRIZE NOT YET DETERMINED.
RITA'S PRIZE ALSO NOT YET DETERMINED.

I lost the contest, 22 to 1. At least one person had taste.

□ □ □

But back to work. Navy Secretary John Lehman was a Naval Reserve pilot who flew out of the Willow Grove Naval Air Station, in suburban Philadelphia. He called a meeting at NADC (Naval Air Development Center) in Warminster, PA. I was a major funder of experiments there. It also contained the centrifuge on which the original seven astronauts trained. John Glenn was in that group. Lehman's meeting involved a subject in which he had great interest: ejection seats. He wanted NADC and NOS (Naval Ordnance Station, Indian Head, Maryland) to develop a common ejection seat. In the world of aviation, "common" means used in two or more kinds of aircraft. Some of the more knowledgeable people in attendance respectfully told the Secretary that was not feasible due to the different cockpit dimensions in different aircraft. Mr. Lehman brushed them aside and told the group to figure it out and get started on it.

I wasn't concerned since I would have no involvement in the design or production of the ejection seat being discussed. Wrong again. Henry Silverman, for whom I had done some work, was put in charge of the project and tapped me to be part of the selection committee to determine who would get the rather lucrative production contract. My part would be the technical documentation for the yet-to-be produced product. It would include the inspection, repair, replacement, challenge and reply checklist, future engineering change proposals, training, stocking of components, including ejection rocketry, the MDC "Mild Detonating Cord" for blowing out the cockpit canopy during ejection, etc.

The selection committee was convened at Jefferson Plaza 2, Naval Air Systems Command Headquarters, Washington, D.C. We met in an airless, secured room. The information from the bidding companies were handed out to each of us according to our so-called areas of expertise. Mine dealt with all technical documentation. We could not talk to each other and could not leave the room without a security guard, even to go to the restroom.

One of the bidders was an English company called Martin Baker located in Chalgrove, England. We were told not to choose that company if it was only for trips to England, because the company had an office in the Washington, D.C. area. The other companies were the usual large, well-known ones such as Boeing, MACAIR, Grumman, Northrop, Stencil etc. After finishing my reviews, which took over six hours, I cast my vote for Martin Baker and took a train back to Philadelphia. It was announced the following week that Martin Baker would get the production contract.

The company was small but had been supplying ejection seats to many countries, including Russia. Baker had died years before, but Martin had been knighted by the Queen of England and was addressed as Sir Martin. Upon receiving word of the successful bid, he threw a large party for his employees at his huge estate. Unfortunately, I did not make the invitation list. However, I did manage to make eleven trips to London Heathrow Airport over the ensuing years. The English whom I dealt with there were charming, polite and friendly, even though I often did not understand them. For example, our car trunks are their boots. Our trucks are their lorries. Flashlights are torches, elevators are lifts, tea with milk is white tea, etc.

□ □ □

I quickly realized that my technical knowledge of ejection seats was pitifully small. I had heard stories of a man who had worked with every single ejection seat ever used by the U.S. Navy and Marine Corps. His name was Doug Scott and he worked at the Naval Air Station, Patuxent River, Maryland. I heard that he was awfully profane and cantankerous and, in general, was disliked. Of course I wanted to meet him, so I called his office and asked his secretary if I could speak to him. She put me on hold.

When she came back, she told me, "Mr. Scott said he does not want to talk to you."

I had heard that he had some problems with someone else in our agency but it had nothing to do with me, so the next day I rented a car and drove to Patuxent River, Maryland, about 45 minutes south of Washington, D.C.

At the gate they looked up Doug Scott for me and said he was located in Hangar 4. Off I went to see the Wizard.

From the map I obtained at the gate, I found Hangar 4, parked, and entered the lion's den. The place was huge, with aircraft wings being moved around, welding, riveting, smells of oil, gas... in short, orchestrated pandemonium. There was a string of offices along a wall but no signs on any of them, so I asked a young man for Mr. Scott's office and followed him there. Inside the office I was met by a large, white-haired lady, his secretary. When I told her my name, she hesitated.

"I just need ten minutes of his time," I said.

She went into his office and quickly came out. "Mr. Scott said ten minutes. No more."

So I entered his office. I expected to see a mess of papers, charts, books, aircraft parts, etc. Instead, I found a meticulously neat office with nothing out of place. Then began the incessant profanity.

"Why the *blankety-blank* did you come here when I said I did not *blankety-blank* want to talk to you? You now have nine minutes. Say your piece and get the *blankety-blank* out of my office!"

I told him that I had heard that he worked on every ejection seat the Navy and Marines ever used.

He said, "You're *blankety-blank* right I have."

Then I referred to the fact that he obviously ran the whole hangar.

"You're *blankety-blank* right I do."

Then I reassured him that it was obvious that he ran a tight and well-oiled operation.

"Play your *blankety-blank* card. You have eight minutes."

So I played my card. "Mr. Scott, you have so much knowledge of ejection seats, yet I run the seat programs, including the new NACES one coming from England. You have all the knowledge, but I have the authority. Let's join forces."

He wanted to know how that would help him.

I told him that if he felt current policy directives were wrong or needed revisions, he could tell me and I would change things to suit him. Since I hadn't heard a curse in over a minute, I assumed I hit pay dirt. I mentioned that either I would have him join me on my business trips, or he could go alone representing me and providing me with notes and meeting minutes.

Now it was time for the coup de grace.

"Mr. Scott, you could shape ejection seat policy all over the world, wherever a Navy or Marine aircraft flies. Look, Doug... may I call you Doug?"

"Shit no, you can't. Your time is up. Bye."

I returned to Philadelphia convinced that there was little or no chance that Mr. Scott would join my team, the old cantankerous bastard.

I was wrong. He eventually called and told me that he was willing to give me a chance. Very big of him. I told him that all I wanted him to do was give me opinions as questions arose on the new NACES ejection seat. At first I did not mention him attending an occasional meeting for me. I just could not see him with those proper Englishmen; he was much too rough a character. I just wanted him to be available to me for advice on maintenance of the seat.

On one occasion I bumped into him in St. Louis at an F-18 meeting. That night, he introduced me to his wife, Isabella. She was as smooth as he was rough, a mannerly schoolteacher who taught English. We sat around a swimming pool where she apologized for her husband's profanity. She said that after a while she didn't really hear it anymore.

For a while things went along fine with Doug advising me on typical ejection seat issues. He also advised me on the fact that the new NACES seat could be easily be adapted to fit into certain aircraft but not all fighters. I passed the information on up the chain of command, and it was acceptable to Secretary Lehman. Then I started to use Doug at any meeting where I was not scheduled to give a presentation just so he could watch my back. That worked fine until he retired from the government and took a job as part-time consultant for the Naval Air Development Facility, an organization which I funded for technical manuals for parachutes, oxygen and flight suits. I still saw Doug at meetings now and then and was aware that he had chemo for throat cancer. Eventually he quit working and retired in Hollywood, Maryland.

One day, I received a call from his wife, Isabella. She said Doug had died and had told her to call me at work and tell me that I was OK. High praise, indeed. RIP Doug, and stop cursing the angels. It's not nice.

□ □ □

On my very first trip to London, I took an overnight flight that landed about 7 or 8 AM local time. After retrieving my luggage, I headed for the car rental area. I had been told which one to use. To my pleasant surprise, when I mentioned my name they handed me a package from Martin Baker containing information and directions to a town called Gerard Cross. When I got in my rental car, I noticed that the shift was floor-mounted, and on my left side. The steering wheel was on what is the passenger side in the US. As I exited Heathrow Airport, I almost immediately came to a "roundabout," which we call traffic circle. The traffic going around the roundabout was entering counterclockwise as opposed to clockwise in the US. I was getting nervous and had to switch off the radio so I could concentrate on not getting myself killed in a foreign country.

Driving on the "wrong side" of the road was a bit disconcerting, too. I pulled over to the side of the road and read the directions to Gerard Cross. In England they do not say something like "take Route 95." They say, "Take the 95." My instructions said to "take the 40." Up ahead I saw a road sign that had the number 40 on it, so I took it. Mistake. In the US, the speed limit signs have *mph* after the speed limit number; in jolly olde England, they just have the number. That's right, I was mistaking their speed limit signs for route numbers. Somehow I eventually arrived at Gerard Cross, found the hotel where I would be staying and parked the car, vowing that I would not get into it again until I was leaving for the airport the following week.

The inn was small and quaint, with only about twenty rooms in it. The woman at the front desk was pleasant and helpful and referred to me as "Yank." There was no computer at the front desk, just one of those old, thick books where guests sign in. As I was completing the signing-in, a familiar face came in. It was a woman named Rowena. When she was an intern in Washington, NAVAIR sent her to our Philadelphia office for some training before returning to Washington. She later was transferred to Bristol, England as a contracting officer, and her Bristol office was going to handle the contractual matters on this new program. We agreed to have breakfast together in the inn's downstairs breakfast room to, as she put it, "get our ducks in order."

The next morning I went downstairs and spotted Rowena sitting alone with a cup of coffee. When I joined her, a waiter came over and asked what I would like for breakfast. I said just coffee. He pointed at the small two-cup container of coffee that Rowena had. I asked for my own coffee. He would not do it. I stood up and moved to the next open table. The same waiter came and once again asked what I wanted for breakfast. Once again I said coffee. He brought me the same kind of two-cup container of coffee Rowena had. I picked it up and rejoined Rowena. Odd people, those Brits.

Later that morning, we were given a tour of their production facilities. Everything was spotless, and we were shown the various ejection seats they had produced for other countries. They explained that for the United States, the seat would have the capability to, upon ejection, sense its position, rotate if necessary to an upright position, and if preprogrammed for a mission over an ocean, drop a line with a salt water sensor into the water, unhook the pilot from his chute and cook a dinner of prime rib and mashed potatoes. (I made up that last part.)

I was told that, as the "tech pub" guy, I would be teamed up with their tech pub guy (a former Royal Air Force pilot) to ensure we were getting exactly what the contract called for. He was a fine lad who had what could be called a drinking problem. His knowledge of ejection seats, not to mention aircraft, was astounding. His wife had recently run off with his good friend, but not before draining their bank account. He mentioned that he had never been to the States and was anxious to come to the capital of Pennsylvania: Philadelphia. I should have told him that this was the first time I had been in the capital of England: Oxford. He was nice enough to ask if I would be interested in seeing the grave of William Penn and seemed stunned when I declined.

Sometime later, an ejection seat meeting was being held in New Orleans, one of my favorite places. I took my son, Brian, with me. At a dinner in the hotel, Brian told the hostess on the side that I had been recently released from a mental facility and asked her to treat me kindly. She would stop by our table from time to time and ask me if everything was OK and could she get me anything. He only told me about it after we left for home.

The next morning as I was signing out before heading to the airport, Alan, the former RAF pilot tech pub guy, came in through the hotel lobby door. I greeted him and asked if he was returning from breakfast. He said, "Oh no, I've been out all night, just coming back in. Quite a town, quite a town!"

On my second business trip to England, I had to go to the Martin Baker production plant. I decided to skip trying to drive on the "wrong" side of the road and just take a train since a train station was only about a half-mile from the plant. After getting off the train, I began walking toward the plant. The weather was quite cold with moderate but steady rain, and it became very windy. When I arrived at the facility and approached Security, the man at the gate had a big smile on his face which I interpreted as a gesture of friendliness for a "Yank" visitor. He directed me toward Building 4, just a short, if wet, cold and windy, walk away.

When I entered the conference room I was met by Angela, a friend from our Norfolk, Virginia office. She took one look at me, laughed and told me to go to the men's room and look in the mirror. I did, and what I saw was a drenched man with wind-blown hair frozen into a mohawk. Angela knocked on the door and asked me not to do anything to my hair until she took a picture of it. I did not comply with that request.

□ □ □

On a more serious note, once again in New Orleans in 1989, I was scheduled to give a talk to the New Orleans Navy Air National Guard. The subject was a new method of supplying pilots with oxygen. It consisted of having molecular sieves in the wings of the AV-8B Harrier aircraft. When air passed over the sieves, only oxygen could be absorbed, no nitrogen or other gasses. When the sieves were saturated with oxygen in one wing, the aircraft automatically switched over to the other wing to enable the O_2 saturation in that wing. The idea was to eliminate oxygen tanks from the cockpit so that a stray enemy bullet could not hit and explode the oxygen tanks.

Anyway, the previous night while in bed, I had a lot of pain and could not lie down; I had to sit in a chair. Whenever the pain would ease up I would climb back in bed, only to have the pain intensity return. This went on all night. It never entered my alleged mind to call the front desk for help. Finally my phone rang with my morning wake-up call. However, I hadn't slept at all. After dressing, I proceeded downstairs to the meeting room. As soon as I walked in, a friend from NADC (Naval Air Development Center) looked at me and told me I looked awful. I thanked him and joined my English co-workers. They kept up the litany of how awful I looked until I began to suspect that I might look awful. That's the scientific mind at work. Somehow, I got through my presentation and excused myself. I decided to fly home a day early.

At home, I made an appointment with our family doctor. He ran an EKG on me and told me to immediately go to Chester County Hospital to see a cardiologist named Vaganos. I did so, and Dr. Vaganos quickly ran tests. He concluded that I had suffered a heart attack while in New Orleans. When I inquired about what to do about it, he said that since I had had the attack and survived, there was not anything we could do about it now except to take steps to avoid it recurring, including angioplasty. That was a procedure where a deflated balloon was inserted through the groin and into the aorta and inflated. It was scheduled to be done at Medical College of Pennsylvania, just three miles from my office in Philadelphia. I was given a local anesthetic and could see what was happening by viewing the same TV screen the surgeon was using. It went well and I went home a couple of days later.

At home in West Chester, Easter 1986

Mom's Demise

In February, 1987, while at the Philadelphia International Airport waiting for a flight to Dayton, Ohio to attend a meeting, I thought I heard my name over the PA system. A short time later,

I heard it again, asking me to contact the operator for an important message.

The message was to call home. My mother was in poor health, and I knew immediately that I had to go to her in Florida. She had been found alive but unconscious on her kitchen floor by a cousin who had stopped in to visit. She had been taken to a hospital in New Port Richey, Florida.

I immediately called Bernadette in the office, who handled all my travel arrangements, and explained the situation to her. She asked me for the number of the phone from which I was calling and told me to stay by that phone. A short time later, she called back and told me that she had cancelled my flight to Dayton, Ohio on USAir, and booked me on an Eastern Airline flight to Tampa, Florida. She had transferred my funding to the Tampa flight and erased all the Dayton information from the federal computer system. The only catch was that the Tampa flight was ready to take off and was leaving from a different terminal. She got them to agree to wait for me.

I spotted a man with a motorized cart and had him take me to the next terminal. Someone waved for me to hurry on board, and as soon as I was buckled in my seat, we pushed back from the gate and took off for Tampa.

Upon arrival, I took a cab to the hospital where Mom was. My brothers, Mick and Jim, were at Mom's bedside.

After my brothers and I discussed my mother's situation with the attending doctor, it was clear that her situation was hopeless and she appeared to be in considerable pain, so we requested that she be administered morphine to keep her comfortable. The doctor refused, citing possible morphine addiction, which, given her hopeless situation, was absurd. The three of us pressed the doctor to reconsider. To increase the pressure, Mickey and Jim were in front of him and I stayed behind him. That seemed to make him nervous, especially since whenever he turned to look at or talk to me, I moved out of his sight, which only increased his nervousness. Eventually he agreed to administer a morphine drip to our mother and she was without pain until she passed away.

In the meantime, there were always one, two or all three of us there 24/7 for over a week. One night when I was "on duty," the room was dark and I was in a chair by her bed.

All of a sudden, in a strong, clear voice, she said, "I want you to stop smoking."

"OK."

She said, "That's it, 'OK'?"

I said, "Yes, I will stop smoking."

She never spoke again. At her request, her body was cremated and her ashes spread over the Gulf of Mexico.

Not long afterward, while walking on the beach during a business trip to Laguna Beach, California, it occurred to me that in that dark hospital room, Mom might have thought that it was Jim sitting there with her. She had often told Jim not to smoke cigarettes and that his father had died of lung cancer. I had been smoking an occasional pipe, not cigarettes.

In fact, I had an urge to smoke a pipe on that beach. I found a drugstore and bought a cheap corncob pipe and a pack of Captain Black tobacco, and bummed some matches from the clerk. While again walking on the beach, smoking the pipe, I noticed that every so often, along the beach, there were large trash cans. I figured that even if Mom thought I was Jimmy, it was I who had promised her that I would stop smoking. I threw the corncob pipe, tobacco and matches in a trash can and never smoked again.

Pooch Stories

My business trips continued. Although I loved New Orleans, the cuisine, the jazz, the ambience, it evidently did not like me. On another business trip there, my wife, Joan, accompanied me. My brother, Mickey, lived in nearby Slidell, and he told us that he knew a real Cajun who lived in the bayou and hunted alligators. Mick told us the Cajun had a boat and could take us on a tour through the bayou to see some alligators. For some reason, we thought that was a good idea. Wrong!!!

A visit to Mickey in Louisiana.
I liked the crabs more than the alligators.

As we snaked through the maze of the bayou, the water level was high due to recent rains. Our guide mentioned that normally we would see alligators sunning themselves on the sandy shore, but due to the high water level, they would be in the water.

Then we hit a log, and I went into that water. The others were not affected by the collision with the log and remained in the boat. The bayou felt very cold, but that was the last thing on my mind. I recalled our guide telling us to be on the look-out for alligators in the water; I opted not to look. The guide maneuvered the boat back to me and told me to hold onto the side while he got us closer to shore. Eventually we got to a tree that had a limb which grew over the water. I climbed up on that limb and jumped back into the boat.

That little adventure created some untrue, but funny stories. I told people that my wife kept yelling for me to throw her the plane tickets and my wallet. Brother Mickey claimed that he kept hitting me with an oar, but I got back into the boat anyway. I believe we still have some pictures taken during the episode. For my coworkers at the office, it provided just another of the many "Pooch" travel stories.

(Pooch was what most people at the office called me. As I've described, I started working for the Feds in 1978, fresh out of research laboratories and completely confounded by the enormous pile of regulations, procedures, acronyms, different "colors" of money, etc. Therefore, during my early days with the agency, I tended to be very quiet and non-communicative, as well as my normal non-smiling self. As a result, I was tagged with the nickname "Mad Dog." After a short time exposed to my particular style of humor and understatement, the moniker "Mad Dog" seemed absurd, and in reference to my somewhat sloppy way of dressing -- and my plaid pants -- I started to be called "Gucci Poochie." That name eventually morphed into "the Pooch." So, for the last 35 or so years, I have been called simply the Pooch.)

OK, here are some more of those Pooch stories I know you are dying to hear.

His Pants Are Falling Down!

On a hot July day, I drove to the Lakehurst, New Jersey Naval Air Station to give some sort of presentation. The venue was a converted movie theater with a stage. I stayed overnight in the BOQ (Bachelor Officer Quarters). The next morning, while putting on a suit and tie, I discovered that I had forgotten to pack a belt. Since I had no time to buy one in Lakehurst, I just went to the meeting place, signed in and headed for the coffee. I noticed that my pants kept slipping down a little, but I kept my left arm close to my side to hold them up, and it seemed to be working.

The stage had a number of metal folding chairs for the visiting dignitaries behind the podium. I sat in the first row of the audience, in front of the stage, awaiting my turn to talk. I was sitting next to a female naval officer. While chatting with her, I asked if she knew this guy on the agenda, Paul Polka.

"Never heard of him," she said.

"He's boring as hell and seldom knows what he's talking about."

She thanked me for the information and said that maybe she would go out for a smoke when it got to him.

Then my name was introduced. As I stood up to climb the stairs to the stage, I heard the female naval officer hiss, "You bastard!"

It was hot on stage, and I was perspiring copiously. As I started my talk, I felt my pants slipping down. I spread my legs slightly apart to stem the slippage. It did not work. I sweated some more, and my pants slipped more. Every time I spread my legs farther apart, I disappeared more and more from behind the microphone. Then, from behind me, I heard one of the honored guests say, "My God, he's losing his pants!" At least I didn't have teddy bear underwear on.

Pooch Gets a Driving Lesson

Another time, I visited El Toro Navy Base in California (now closed). When I went to rent a car, they said they were out of compact cars, which by law I had to rent. They said I could have any other kind and only pay the compact rate, so I chose a large Lincoln Continental. The car was loaded with things such as indoor/outdoor thermometer, gas consumption rate, power everything including seats, etc. I wasn't used to all that.

When I arrived at El Toro, I was stopped by a very young-looking Marine at the gate. It was about 8AM, so there were many cars lined up to get to their jobs. As usual, I held up my travel orders for him to see. He motioned for me to roll down my window, but I could not find the darn window switch. I would push some button and the driver's seat would move forward. Another button, and it'd move backward. Another button, and windshield wipers turned on. Another, and the trunk lid popped open. I finally just opened my door. With horns honking behind me, the Marine yelled at me to pull over, out of the way of people trying to get to work, and learn how my car worked before continuing on. I said, "Yes, sir" to the kid Marine, albeit a kid Marine with a .45 caliber pistol.

Pooch Gets an Eyeful

Our technical director, a GS-15, was going to IBM in Manassas, Virginia and asked me to go along. After checking into a hotel, he told me of a restaurant nearby that was originally a Catholic church. A little fearful I would be struck down by a bolt of lightning upon entering the restaurant, I decided to join him. Done eating, we started to walk back to our hotel.

As we stood waiting at a traffic light, a car pulled up beside us. There was a young girl driving and another one slunk down in the passenger seat. Just as the light turned green, the one in the passenger seat sat up and stuck both of her breasts out the window and started yelling, "Whoohoo! Whoohoo!" as they drove away.

Now, that was all that really happened, but on several occasions afterward, while recounting the incident to some people, the technical director would always add that I started to run after the girls while shouting my hotel room number. Untrue. Good idea, but untrue.

Flag Waving for Pooch

At MCAS (Marine Corps Air Station) Cherry Point, North Carolina, I had to give a presentation on some AV-8B Harrier aircraft. As I worked my way through the presentation, every once in a while a Marine seated near the front would wave a flag attached to the end of a slender bamboo pole. Each time he did that, many of the attendees grunted approval and amens.

After the flag was raised and waved about three times, I asked what it meant.

A Marine in the back stood up and shouted, "It's our bullshit flag. Whenever we hear bullshit, we wave the bullshit flag!"

Pooch's Celebrity Sighting

I often took a train to meetings in Washington, D.C. On one of those trains a woman was sitting across from me, and she looked familiar. She was writing something, and I saw a folder with the call letters WHYY on it. Then it hit me: it was Charlayne Hunter-Gault from the Jim Leher News Hour on Channel 12.

I asked her if she was indeed Miss Hunter-Gault, and she said she was and that she was returning to Washington from somewhere in New England. I told her that I was a good friend of Jim Leher and to please tell him that Paul Polka said hello. She said she would do that and wrote my name down. I don't know if she ever told him, but if she did, he probably scratched his head wondering who the heck this Paul Polka was.

Pooch Holds It Together

While at work one day, I heard a ripping noise when I bent over. No, it wasn't escaping gas; it was a tear in the crotch of my pants. What to do? (I did not want all the secretaries to get too excited.) Then I had what I thought was a great idea. I took a stapler into the men's room and very carefully stapled the tear closed with several staples and put my pants back on. Everything seemed to be working fine, but when I sat back down at my desk, I felt a rather sharp pain. I returned to the men's room once again and discovered that I had stapled the pants with the pointy ends inside instead of outside. Well, it was almost a great idea.

Pooch and the Nail File

One of our office secretaries called me at my desk one day and asked if I had a nail file. I did not, but it gave me an idea. The next day I brought in a large nail from home and put it in a plain manila folder marked "Nail File."

It took about three or four months, but finally a different secretary asked me if I had a nail file.

"Yes, I do," I said.

I pulled out the manila folder and handed it to her. She opened it, saw the nail and almost collapsed laughing while calling me a "crazy SOB."

Pooch and the Ring of Protection

Some time ago, the fantasy game of Dungeon & Dragons was very popular, and at work, a group of four or five of us played the game during lunch. There was a Dungeon Master with whom you could have secret conversations. During one of those conversations, I told the Dungeon Master that I possessed a "Ring of Protection." The Dungeon Master told me that it could only be used to save my life once.

During the course of the game, I told another player in confidence that I had the "Ring of Protection" and would sell it to him in exchange for his fast horse. I also told him that he could verify through the Dungeon Master that I indeed had the ring. What he did not know is that I had told the Dungeon Master that I had a fake "Ring of Protection," too, which was the one I sold to my unsuspecting fellow player. When that player was in danger of being slain, he proclaimed that he was protected by the ring.

The Dungeon Master said, "It doesn't work. You bought a fake ring."

Everyone laughed, except the victim of the con job, who ironically was the agency's Financial Director.

Pooch Ties One On

I had been to Grumman in Bethpage, New York a few times with my original supervisor, but I finally was sent alone to hold a contract meeting involving the E-2C surveillance aircraft. Marge, my supervisor, told me to be firm with them regarding delivery and their contractual obligations. I was nervous, but the meeting went well, with me maintaining a serious, no-nonsense tone. I ended the meeting and stuffed my papers into my briefcase, not realizing that I was stuffing my tie in along with them. I closed the briefcase with my tie caught in it, and as I pulled it off the table, it threw me off balance, almost causing me to fall. So much for making a good impression.

Pooch Discovers an Interest in Botany

Sometime around Easter 1978, when Joan was feeling down and blue, I thought of taking her and the kids to see a bush that I had spotted which had multicolored buds on it, some blue, some green, some pink and even some yellow. It seemed to me to be quite unusual, and with her interest in plants, I thought seeing it would lift her spirits.

She was intrigued, so all of us jumped in the car while I hoped I could remember where the remarkable bush was. After a short drive I spotted it and proudly drove up to it, asking if Joan knew what it was. Yes, she did. It was a bush that had various colored pieces of egg carton attached to its twigs. I was embarrassed that I had thought it was a bush with different colored buds, but it did accomplish my aim to lift Joan's spirit. She still laughs about the *Eggus Cartonius* today.

Chapter Seven

NATEC

In 1993 the BRAC (Base Relocation And Closure) Commission was convened. It consisted of seven non-partisan members. The non-partisan part is an oxymoron, much like "honest politician." It was later determined that there never has been the closure of a base in any member's state. Anyway, NATSF was being considered for closure. We fought it very vigorously, led by Glen Weder, our Financial Officer. The BRAC voted 7 - 0 not to close us.

Fast forward to 1995: the BRAC people who a few years earlier voted 7-0 in our favor suddenly voted 7-0 to close us. In fact, that commission not only voted to relocate us, but to replace us with a wholly different organization, something called NATEC (Naval Air Technical Engineering Command). The new Technical Director was going to be a woman who, it was later discovered, was an intimate friend of the same SES (Senior Executive Service) man who wanted to close NATSF. A mere coincidence, I'm certain. The new facility would be located on Coronado Island, across the bay from San Diego. The transition was ordered to be accomplished by October 1st, 1998, the beginning of the federal fiscal year. We were ordered by the SES guy to offer training for our replacements, but the Civil Service Commission determined that any NATSF employee who wanted to work 3,000 miles away would have to be hired.

I considered retiring, but knew I had other options open to me: I could wait to be picked up by another federal agency, I could comb various openings in other agencies closer than 3,000 miles, I could return to non-federal employment, or I could retire. When word of NATSF's impending demise spread, I started to get phone calls from several other agencies. Fort Belvoir, Virginia called and wanted me to get involved in their night vision goggles research. Naval Weapons Center, China Lake, California offered me a position working on the propulsion sled used to test ejection seat rocket assemblies. It all made me feel confident that I would not be out on the street with no options.

However, in typical Paul style, I relished the thought of going to San Diego, where I was told in no uncertain terms by the TD (Technical Director), Linda, that I was not wanted. When I considered various financial, personal and health problems, it seemed to beckon me.

I hammered out details with Human Resources. They agreed to ship my car cross-country, pay for my plane ticket to the West Coast, pay for a rental car for three months, a room at the Ferry Landing Hotel on Coronado for three months and reimbursement for all food for three months. The only catch was that I had to sign a "mobile agreement" that I agreed to stay in San Diego for at least three years. If I did not, I would have to reimburse the federal government for all monies paid to me during those three months. That would be many thousands of dollars. In case you are wondering, I stayed for the three-year minimum.

◻ ◻ ◻

When I officially checked in at NATEC, I was approached by the Technical Director's chief henchman, a dope named Joe. He did not welcome me. He just mentioned that the TD, Linda, wanted to know what program I wanted to manage. BOING!!! *Program*, as in singular. In Philly I had eight to ten programs to

La Jolla, California, 2000

manage -- the number varied -- though some were active and some were not very. One program would be a piece of cake. My big problem would be how to kill the spare time. Anyhow, I told the henchman that I wanted Survival. He just turned around and went upstairs to the Queen's office, then returned and told me that Queenie said OK. I was in.

My desk at first had no phone, no file cabinet and no computer. Those were all provided little by little. It was all placed in a small cubicle, and I settled in. Survival included oxygen, flight suits, ejection seats, test sets, armament, HUD (Heads Up Display), survival radios, special glasses to combat laser beams, decoding equipment and parachutes. Travel requirements were minimal. A typical work day began with an early commute in order to beat the rush hour traffic over the Coronado Bridge. I'd stop at the Burger King at the ferry landing, get coffee and a newspaper, do the crossword puzzle, then drive onto the Air Station and go to my desk. The pace was soooooo not frantic.

The Little Red Road

In December 2000, daughter Bridget decided to leave her home in Queens, New York and join me in San Diego while she job-hunted there. I was home on annual leave for the holidays, and she wanted me to drive a U-Haul truck that we loaded in New York back to California.

We drove from Queens back to our house in West Chester, Pennsylvania, then left West Chester the following morning and headed south toward Atlanta, intending to visit a friend there and stay overnight.

We watched the miles tick by... and the pavement, too, through the gaping hole in the floor. Bridget finally stuffed a towel into it so we wouldn't have to watch the miles pass by quite so literally. Then we heard a funny noise, but eventually it went away. Unfortunately, so did the brakes.

That's when we pulled over and attempted our first rescue via AAA, only having made it about 20 miles from home. Although the disabled truck was situated by the side of the road, not more than fifty yards from the toll booths at the entrance to I-95, the tow truck driver claimed he could not find us. It took so long that I suggested setting the sofa on fire atop the truck to help them find us, but Bridget refused. Eventually the tow truck driver managed to locate a large U-Haul truck sitting on the shoulder of a major highway very near well-lit toll booths, much as we had said repeatedly. He drove us to what had to be the worst U-Haul franchise for miles... and missed the exit. No problem. He backed the tow truck and our truck up on the highway. Then, at the franchise, there followed arguments, phone calls, in-person glaring contests and more, finally leading to a fixed truck and a very low opinion of the franchise's service. What a terrific beginning to a 3,000 mile trip.

Bridget, Clarence and I outside Atlanta, GA, January, 2000

We stopped in Atlanta as planned and stayed with friends overnight. Then we hit the road again, taking the southern route toward California.

By this time, Bridget and I had named our truck Clarence, because we "misread" the word *clearance* on the side of the truck.

At a rest stop somewhere just inside Louisiana, Clarence was reluctant to start up again, despite my cursing. I pleaded with a couple of other drivers for a jump, but alas, no luck. Amazingly, however, when Bridget did the pleading, we got help. Further on down the road, I thought it best to have someone check the battery. We pulled into a Sears auto repair shop where a nice man raised the hood and asked what I thought was a strange question: "Which battery do you want checked?" That's how I found out for the first time that the truck had two, count 'em, two batteries. Clarence never mentioned that fact, and we had jumped the right battery just by chance. Anyway, we purchased a new battery and went on our way.

Early on, we had discovered that Clarence balked at restarting if the engine cooled down too much. Whenever we stopped for something to eat, we left the engine running while we ate, keeping an eye on the idling truck. The refueling plan, then, was that whenever we stopped to give Clarence a drink of diesel fuel, I would hop out of the truck and Bridget would slide behind the steering wheel. With the engine off, I would pump the fuel and as soon as I finished pumping, I would bang on the side of the truck, which was the signal for Bridget to quickly turn on the ignition while I went inside to pay. If we were fast enough, Clarence would not have time to cool down enough to refuse to start. It always worked.

□ □ □

While driving at night through Texas, we spotted a brightly-lit gas station a short distance off the highway. I wanted to make a call back home and use a restroom, so we took that exit. When we got to the gas station, it was very brightly-lit but totally deserted. No cars refueling, none parked, not a soul in sight. It was as if everyone had just stepped away for a minute, but the place was so isolated, there were no other businesses around for miles. It really was creepy, and both Bridget and I felt extremely edgy. It had an outside payphone, so I got out of the truck and told Bridget to get behind the wheel and be ready to quickly get away from there.

I tried the door to the men's room. It was locked. The door to the ladies' room was open just a little, with a light on. It occurred to me that it could be an open invitation for some unsuspecting woman, but it was so small that I could quickly inspect it for a possible intruder. I used the restroom, made a brief call home, and quickly got back into the truck. There still was nobody we could see, the station was still brightly lit and there were still no cars. We departed quickly for the main highway, both of us feeling there was an evilness to the place, and we were very happy to return to the open road.

□ □ □

When we crossed over into New Mexico, we stopped at a rest stop and Bridget asked if she could take my picture next to a sign that I figured said something like, "Welcome To New Mexico." Instead, as I found out when I saw the picture, it read, "Watch For Snakes."

I was getting the impression that New Mexico didn't like us, but we decided to stop at a Chinese restaurant anyway. That was a good idea except that I misjudged Clarence's height and rammed into the corrugated metal roof of the restaurant, making an ugly crunching sound. The only other sound I heard was Bridget yelling "Go, go, go!" I went, quickly pulling out on the road again.

Foolishly, I figured nothing else could happen to us in New Mexico. Wrong again. After a rest stop, we wanted to get back on the big interstate highway. Bridget consulted a map and said we could save time and miles by taking "this little red road" to connect with the interstate. So we took the "little red road." It turned out to be a narrow two-way road with patchy ice here and there, hairpin turns, no guard rail and a steep cliff always just inches away from the edge of the road with our oversized truck always perilously close to going off it. We could not turn around into oncoming traffic, so we crossed our clenched fingers and kept going. Eventually, the damn "little red road" ended and we joined up with the elusive interstate.

Finally we made it to San Diego.

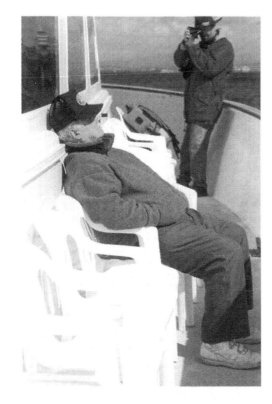

On a whale watching trip off the San Diego coastline… wasn't anyone actually watching for whales???

Back to Work

One of my favorite memories from San Diego involved Joe, the henchman. I sometimes have the habit of parking where I shouldn't, and I did that on the base from time to time. Joe Bozo would enjoy jumping on me about it. He took special pains to check on my parking situation, hoping to take me to task about it.

One day he came into my cubicle and motioned for me to follow him to the side entrance, where he pointed out a tow truck towing a car away. Bozo asked what I thought of that.

I said something like, "Why show me a car being towed?"

"I'm tired of telling you not to park illegally, so I called for the tow truck to take your car away."

"That's not my car."

It was the same model Mercury Tracer that I had, but my car had Pennsylvania license plates and that car had California plates.

I left him with, "Sorry, shithead."

The story made the rounds, and I never illegally parked in front of the office again so that I would not give him the satisfaction of having my car towed for real.

The Great Picture Caper, or OK, Who Took It?

One day my friend, Ebbie, walked quickly by my cubicle carrying a load of papers. I heard, "Psst! Come with me."

We went out the door to the parking lot.

"Where's your car?"

I pointed it out and followed her there.

"Open the trunk."

I did, and she dug into the stack of papers in her arm, pulling out the TD's picture. I protested that I would be the prime suspect.

She laughed, and said, "I know." She put the picture in the trunk and closed it.

The very next morning, I was told that the CO wanted to see me. Gee, what a surprise! I went upstairs without even glancing at the wall where the pictures of top management were. In the office, the CO and Linda Loosescrew were waiting for me. The CO wasted no time.

"Did you take the picture?"

"Picture? What picture?" Evidence of my Pittston upbringing.

"Linda's picture!!"

More Pittston kicked in. He did not ask if I had it, or even if I knew who did have it, just if I had taken it. With a pained, hurt look on my face, I told the truth.

"No, sir, I definitely did NOT take it."

I turned around and left indignantly without being excused. At the bottom of the steps, Ebbie was waiting expectantly. I told her that I was suspended, then relented. "Not really."

At the time this all occurred, daughter Bridget was living with me. When I showed her the picture, she took it and retouched it to show Linda's blouse with convict stripes and a prisoner number on it, and handcuffs on her wrists. A brilliant job, indeed. I decided to donate the picture to Glenn Weder, our former financial officer who spearheaded our successful fight against closure the first time. My old NATSF coworkers get together every October for a reunion luncheon, and Glenn always brings the picture to the luncheons. The now-infamous picture is always prominently displayed, much to everyone's delight. Bridget is somewhat famous for her artistic flair, at least within our group.

At the Coronado Ferry Landing in 2000

□ □ □

Linda and I continued exhibiting our deep dislike for each other. I was totally disengaged from her, and she normally had nothing to do with me. Frankly, she had no clue as to what my job really consisted of, which was fine with me. Occasionally she called for an "All Hands" meeting. I never attended them. Her top henchman, Joe, told me that "All Hands" meant ALL HANDS, but of course I still refused to attend if she was the one calling for the meetings.

In fact, I did pretty much as I pleased at work. Linda had done a good job of poisoning the well, which resulted in most of the NATEC employees avoiding the "NATSF guy." Also, they felt it would not be smart to fraternize with someone the big boss did not like. That started to change when a data manager named Jackie Goodman complained to my good friend Ebbie that she had two meetings convening at the same time and could not cover both of them. Ebbie suggested she ask me to cover one of them for her. Jackie told her that first of all it was at Marine Air Station, North Carolina; secondly, it concerned the Air Force C-130J, which I knew nothing about (true); and finally, why would a NATSF guy help someone he didn't know and who was part of "the enemy?" Ebbie told her that I really didn't need to know what I was talking about.

Anyway, Jackie must have been desperate, because she came to me with her dilemma and asked if I would help. I said, "Sure," then asked her to get me her files, contracts and minutes of other C-130J meetings. She did, and I knew I could handle it sufficiently well enough to help her since the background stuff was mostly standard procedures of funding, documentation, etc. For the final step, I asked her to tell me what the program's most pressing problem was. She told me, sheepishly, that she had no clue how to write a TMCR (Technical Manual Contract Requirement) or how to get it incorporated. I told her that I would write it and bring it to Cherry Point, North Carolina. She almost cried, and asked what I wanted in return. I told her it would cost her a can of Pepsi.

One result of all that was that she went from not wanting to have anything to do with the "NATSF guy" to asking me to take a walk with her when she did her exercise stroll most afternoons. Her husband, who worked for an airline at the San Diego airport, had hurt his back so badly that they moved their bedroom to the first floor so he would not have to negotiate the stairs, and she wanted to stay in shape to be able to care for him.

By the way, the North Carolina meeting went just fine, as I did my well-practiced Pooch tap dance. You know, the one I did at Marine meetings, where as I was introduced, the Chair would say "Music, maestro, please."

Pooch Breaks the Captain's Chair

The NATEC office was originally a building where helicopters were repaired. It was renovated to become our office.

You might say it had a decent location. On our left was the Pacific Ocean and on the right, San Diego Harbor. Air conditioning was not necessary. A chain-link fence separated us from the dock, where there usually was an aircraft carrier moored not more than 100 feet away. In July, 2000, son Brian visited me, and I arranged for a private tour of the USS Stennis carrier. There were no personnel aboard the Stennis, but a Navy senior chief took us aboard. He showed us the elevator that could take a fighter from the repair shop up to the top deck in something like three seconds. On top, Brian noticed large rubber nets on both sides of the deck. The chief explained that when there was a crash imminent or a big problem with a landing, the sailors would jump into those nets.

We got to the helm, where the ship's captain sat. Brian told me to hop up on the captain's "sacred" chair so he could take a picture of me. I was considerably larger (fat) at the time, and the chair was high to give the captain a good view of all the ship activity. There was a metal ring around the bottom of the chair, and as I stepped on the ring in order to give myself a heave up, the chair broke. *The captain's chair broke!!!* The Navy chief almost fainted. Brian still took the picture, which I believe he still has.

So, I broke the captain's chair on the magnificent USS Stennis, CVN 74, in port at US Naval Air Station, North Island, California.

"Now We Got Him"

Joe came into my cubicle one day and, with a smirk on his face, told me that I had better relent and come with him to see the Commanding Officer and dear Linda. He insinuated that I was in big trouble. That really did bother me because I didn't always play by the rules. While working hard trying to figure out what they wanted to discuss with me before I got there, I couldn't think of anything I had done that they would even understand. When I arrived in the CO's office, I decided to go on the offensive, not defensive (a trick I learned from my friend, Larry).

"OK, here I am. Make it quick, I'm very busy."

Linda spoke first. She said that she was informed that I used federal money for personal use. I asked for details instead of accusations. Linda then mentioned a pot of money that I placed somewhere where I could use it for personal reasons.

Internally, I breathed a sigh of relief. I knew what they were referring to, so I decided to fire a couple of torpedoes.

I told them that I had an agreement with NPPSO, Lexington, Kentucky, in which I would fund their yearly printing budget for my manuals and add $25,000 to be set aside for me anytime I needed it. So, if their budget for my stuff was $150,000, I would transfer $175,000 with the stipulation that the $25,000 extra could only be tapped into by me for authorized federal travel.

I then said, "For those of you who can read, I can tell you what federal regulations cover that procedure." I looked at Linda. "It's all *exactly* like your 'sweep-up money' that the whole United

States government uses every fourth quarter of every fiscal year. The old 'use it or lose it'."

I ended with, "I have well-documented proof of how every penny was used. Can you say the same?"

I was really steamed. As I stormed out of the office, I heard the CO say, "Dammit, Linda!!"

Oh My God, He Knows Mr. Silverman

I really like this part and hope you will too.

A man named Henry Silverman, someone high up in the Naval Air Command Headquarters, Washington, DC, was coming to NATEC. I knew him from doing some jobs for him in England and a couple of other places, but I had not heard about his coming visit. His star was rising within the government, and there was some excitement about his visit. He arrived during my usual extended lunchtime. When I got back to the office, Linda was leading him down the steps from Mount Olympus, giving him the grand tour.

When they turned at the bottom of the stairs, he spotted me and yelled, "PAUL!!"

I yelled, "Henry!!"

We shook hands and hugged briefly. Linda did not look happy. I was eating up the moment. I told him he looked good and inquired about the gym he had in the basement of his house. He asked if I would have dinner with him at a seafood restaurant on Coronado. I quickly said yes and mentioned that we had a lot to talk about. Linda just kept smiling. I don't think it was lost on her that "Henry" had not invited her to join us. They continued the tour.

My friend Ebbie said something like, "You *expletive, expletive, expletive,* you set this up, didn't you?" I told the truth, which was I had no idea he was coming. She did not *expletive* believe me, but it was true.

We met at the Brigantine Restaurant on Coronado. After a quick "catching up," he got down to business and asked me to tell him about NATEC. I took a chance and told him that I knew that he knew and heard a lot, or he wouldn't be there. I went ahead and told him of their lack of a contract section, lack of employees knowledgeable about technical documentation, and the fact that they had nobody to train them in all the nuances, etc. When I told him about the recent run-in about alleged misuse of government funds, he perked up. He told me that he was tipped off that Linda had used government funds to pay two people to write a paper for her in her pursuit of a master's degree. I said that I knew nothing about that but was not surprised to hear it. I asked him if Linda's job was in jeopardy. He tap-danced the answer; I could almost hear the music in the background. He was still at NATEC for the next day or so, but we did not have any further conversations.

A couple of weeks later, I had to go to Indianapolis for a meeting with the company that made the huge propeller engines for the V-22 Marine aircraft. That plane took off like a helicopter, then flew like a regular plane. A couple of test pilots had been killed while the plane transitioned from vertical to horizontal flight.

While I was there, I found a message waiting for me back at my room one day. It just said, "SHE'S GONE."

It was from Ebbie, and I later found out that Linda was told she would be escorted off the base after normal business hours, taking what personal items she could carry, and any personal items remaining would be sent to her. She was not to enter the base again, even as a guest.

Chapter Eight

Medical

On Thanksgiving Day, 2000, while sitting at the dinner table at my in-laws' home, I suddenly felt odd. Since that was not all that unusual for me, I ignored it and continued eating my turkey dinner. Then, while looking at my father-in-law, something did not seem quite right. I could not figure out exactly what it was, but then it occurred to me: his head was not only where it was supposed to be, it also was in the middle of his chest. Somehow this did not seem right, but I just continued eating my dinner. I looked around and realized that the four of us were actually eight. Now, I had to wrestle with that for a moment. I'm normally very good with numbers, but I could not grasp where all these people came from. Then I said that I did not feel well and was told to lie down in the guest bedroom. After a short time there, I returned to the table and tried to seem normal. It did not fool my wife though, and she demanded that I see an ophthalmologist the very next day.

I reluctantly agreed, and off we went. The ophthalmologist checked me out and determined that I had suffered a brain stem stroke. He also said that what was done was done, but if I had any more symptoms, to quickly go to the ER.

On January 6, 2001 I was acting strangely enough that Joan suggested going to the ER. I stubbornly refused and actually started to sob. That shook her to the extent that she called our son, Brian, and told him what was going on. Brian quickly arrived wearing a silly dreadlock type of wig in an attempt to lighten the mood. It worked, and I was taken to the ER, was given some tests and was told that I had suffered yet another and even worse stroke. I was referred to Bryn Mawr Rehabilitation Hospital, where I stayed for about a month.

Bryn Mawr Rehab is a well-regarded hospital, and I was fortunate to have been sent there. I was placed in a room located in the stroke ward. They scheduled me for occupational therapy, physical therapy and speech therapy. The speech therapist, a great lady named Amy, first wanted to determine if I could swallow solid food. I could, so I was allowed to eat regular food instead of puréed food. Then she began giving me tongue twisters, which produced sounds at first that were, shall we say, unusual. Slowly, I got better at the tongue twisters and continued working on them three days a week.

It was going quite well until at one session, she informed me that my federal health insurance would not pay for my speech therapy any longer. Amy felt badly about it because I was working so hard and making good progress. She thought long and hard about it, then said that she would continue to see me during her lunch break so my therapy would not take place officially at the hospital and no insurance claim would have to be filed. So the therapy continued, thanks to a wonderful lady who worked through lunch for my benefit.

□ □ □

There was some humor even in the stroke ward. On one visit to the hospital my son, Brian, brought me a teddy bear that farted when squeezed. A nurse's aide would wake me up to take my "vitals" at 5 AM. One morning, as she awakened me, I turned over and squeezed the teddy bear, which was under the covers. She politely ignored the rather loud sound, so I moved again while squeezing the toy. The aide laughed and said she had heard about me from some of the other workers.

My bed was wired in a way to set off an alarm in the nurses' station if I attempted to get out of bed unaccompanied. I studied the apparatus and figured out how to disarm it. That worked well until my wife told the nurses about my little trick.

In order to help me get back some of the dexterity in my fingers, a hospital candy striper played cards with me. Of course, she was unaware that I could do a lot of card tricks. We played blackjack, better known as 21. I did the shuffling and cutting. She was amazed at how "lucky" I was.

□ □ □

All this happened while I was on annual leave for the holiday season. Thankfully, I had great health coverage with the federal government and received full pay while convalescing at home. However, I felt I needed to return to my temporary, long-term assignment on the island of Coronado, across the harbor from San Diego, California. My duties consisted of logistical support to Navy Seals, Marine and Navy aviators in the fields of survival, weaponry and chemical warfare. These duties required contracts, meetings, strategy sessions, funding and problem solving. The reason I mention this is because after my second stroke, I did not realize that I had lost some of my prior capabilities. When I arrived back at my desk and started to go through some of the paperwork that had accumulated during my absence, I realized that it took considerably longer to absorb the information than it did prior to my stroke. I could do what was required, but it took longer than it used to. I also got overtired very quickly. It started to dawn on me that, to use a sports cliché, I lost a step, or maybe even two.

Since I worked alone, it probably wasn't noticed that I was a slower study than before. Some close friends felt that I was merely recovering from severe medical problems.

I phoned a former NATSF employee who now worked in Patuxent River Naval Air Station, Patuxent, Maryland. He knew a lot about survival and chemical warfare. I told him that I was tired and weary from various medical problems and asked him if he would like to take over my duties. He agreed to do that, but with the stipulation that he would do it in Maryland, not San Diego, because he abhorred the San Diego Technical Director as much as I did. I agreed and shifted most things to Patuxent River without even notifying Linda.

Eventually, for both medical and personal reasons, I retired. After my last day at NATEC, as I stepped out of the side door leading to my illegally parked car, I paused. I looked past the chain link fence separating the office from the dock, and images flooded my mind. I could see in my mind's eye the carriers that berthed there, the crowds of family and friends coming to greet the sailors after their six- or nine-month deployments. The wives, the girlfriends, the moms holding their infants up high so their daddies could see them, some for the very first time, the Marine or Navy band playing marches, the confetti, the unbridled joy of the forthcoming reunion, the truly magnificent sight of the carrier slowly inching toward the dock with 6,000 or so sailors lined up along the ship's edge, standing at attention in their dress whites but with wide grins on their faces. It was all so fabulous. Why didn't I think of it that way before?

Then, back to the present. No ship, no crowds, no bands, no confetti, no sailors... no Linda.

I walked down to the water's edge and threw my NATEC ID into the bay, and drove back over the Coronado Bridge for the last time. Now I really was going home.

□ □ □

Exactly one year after my second stroke, on January 6th, 2002, Joan and I intended to take our dog, Brandy, for a walk in the township park. When we realized how icy it was, we opted instead to visit Joan's parents in a local assisted living facility.

Once there, I fixed a TV remote for them while Joan was on the floor sorting some of her mother's clothes. I sat in a chair and watched. Evidently I made some sort of sound, and she looked up in time to see my eyes roll back in my head. She grabbed me and pulled me down to the floor, yelled for help, ran to call 911 and then tried to give me CPR. Some staff workers ran into the room and also started CPR, but I was not responding. A short time later, an ambulance crew arrived. They used their portable defibrillator on the regular setting. There was no response from me. They turned up the power all the way and tried again. Joan later told me that my body jumped about an inch off the floor (at the time, I weighed over 200 pounds). The EMTs then injected a needle filled with epinephrine directly into my heart. No response again.

While they tried another needle of heart stimulant, Joan stepped out of the room to call our son, Brian. She told him what was happening and asked him to notify our daughter, Bridget, who lived in Queens, New York. He did, and she immediately packed some clothes and boarded a train to Philadelphia believing that her father was dead. Brian jumped in his car to come to the assisted living facility where all this was happening.

Meanwhile, Joan came back into the room and, kneeling at my feet, told the ambulance crew that she felt a weak, sporadic pulse in my ankle. They rushed my stretcher downstairs and out to the ambulance just as Brian pulled up. Realizing that paramedics don't run for dead people, he stayed in his car and followed the ambulance to the ER, where it was determined that I wasn't quite dead after all. I was taken to the ICU and hooked up to a multitude of wires and electronics. Things looked grim because of how long I had gone without oxygen, but I began to recover. Over the next days, I became more aware of my surroundings and started to respond to people, but it would be quite awhile before I could understand what was going on. Because of my condition, no more than three visitors were allowed. Somehow, there frequently were five or more.

Because I was hooked up to so many machines, I was not allowed to use the bathroom that was right there in the room. I asked daughter Bridget if she would help me get to a bathroom.

To keep me in bed, she said, "The hospital doesn't have any bathrooms."

"Then what do the doctors and nurses use?"

"The gas station down the street."

I accepted that explanation!!

A neurologist stopped in to check on me. He asked if I knew who the president was. My son, Brian, immediately objected to the question, stating that there had been a presidential election a couple of months before, but the winner would not assume office until January 20th.

Then the doctor asked, "Are you married?"

"Yes, I am."

"Is your wife in the room?"

I looked around. "No."

Of course she was right by the bed.

Once Joan wrote my name on a sheet of white paper, in large black letters: PAUL. When asked what was written on the sheet of paper, I said it was blank. My brain could not process the letters.

My family spent a lot of time with me in the ICU, and as I kept showing rapid improvement in brain function, the staff credited my family and their constant banter with me as a tremendous help in my recovery process. In room after darkened ICU room, there were only quiet, hushed murmurs. My room, on the other hand, had talkative visitors engaging me in conversation and humor, all of which proved very therapeutic. My improvement continued, and I was eventually discharged from the hospital to resume the important activities of my retirement, which I shall elucidate for you next. (I know, I know... you do and you clean it up.)

.

Chapter Nine

The Arts

Since retiring, I have had time to devote to more important things, such as sudoku and listening to the radio. I have also pursued the arts, despite a curious lack of patronage. I share with you some of the results here, whether you like it or not.

TERMS OF USE

The viewer of the following original art agrees not to use any part of it for commercial profit without the express written consent of the artist. No part of the art can be reprinted or copied on pain of prosecution by federal authorities under the auspices of Title XX of Public Law 23, Section IV. The showing of the art is forbidden in, of course, New Jersey, any state bordering Idaho, and two or three streets in Scranton. Reprints are available from the Feasterville Volunteer Fire Department, 2nd floor; ask for Jake. The art is suitable for framing by the LAPD.

ABOUT THE ARTIST, AS IF YOU HAVEN'T HEARD ENOUGH ALREADY

The artist was born in a small town in Pennsylvania. Growing up in a house by the busy railroad tracks of the Lehigh Valley Railroad, his fascination with trains began at a young age with throwing rocks at passing trains while laughing hysterically, then moved on to many futile attempts at derailing the sleek new trains of the 1950's by putting pennies on the tracks. His art is completely self-taught, and his signature bold strokes have been the envy of his fellow artists for years. His drawings have not been shown in an impressive array of galleries in this country and abroad. He is most delighted with not having any of his work displayed in the prestigious Museum of Modern Art in New York. Visitors to the famed Tate Museum of London will note that the artist's renditions are not displayed on floor after floor of that institution. Besides those monumental galleries, the artist is not represented at numerous, less well-known galleries in towns across the United States.

Just some of the awards he has not won include, but are not limited to, Best New Artist, Artist to Watch, the Andrew Wyeth Memorial Award, and others too numerous to mention.

Enjoy. Or not.

VERY
ARTISTIC
ARTWORK

Flock of Birds Flying Over a Train

In this drawing, the birds are so detailed, so life-like, that the viewer can almost hear the flapping of their wings.

Boy, With Dog, Waving at Train Engineer

A time-honored tradition is saluted in this thrilling depiction of a youngster giving a wave to the passing train. The skimpy drawing of the lad serves to emphasize the size of the train. The dog who normally accompanied the boy was not there at the time of the drawing and so is not shown.

Pipe Jutting Out From the Front of the Train

A perennial crowd favorite, this drawing illustrates the whimsical side of the artist. Some feel he is comparing the relaxation of a train ride with the relaxation and serenity of pipe smoking. Others, less generous, believe it is an indication of the onset of dementia.

Train Going by Brooklyn Bridge Hidden by Fog

Here, the artist once again manifests his remarkable ability to draw the unseen by showing how the imposing structure of the famed Brooklyn Bridge would look to a train rider if it were foggy.

Train About to Enter a Tunnel (Not Seen)

In this drawing, the artist brilliantly alludes to life's uncertainties as we travel through the landscapes of our lives. Although the viewer cannot see the exquisitely detailed drawing of the railroad tunnel, the artist assures us that it is there in all its rugged glory.

Train After Coming Out of a Tunnel (Not Seen)

In this drawing, the artist brilliantly alludes to life's uncertainties as we travel through the landscapes of our lives. Although the viewer cannot see the exquisitely detailed drawing of the railroad tunnel, the artist assures us that it is there in all its rugged glory.

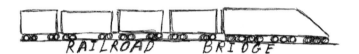

Train Rolling Over a Railroad Bridge

The brilliant use of symbolism highlights this artistic masterpiece. In lieu of the hackneyed depiction of a typical railroad bridge, the artist is able to adroitly utilize text in place of art. This is thought to be an artistic breakthrough showing independence from the trite abstract cubism so favored by those less talented.

Train With Soap Bubbles in Second Car

The reason the artist included soap bubbles in the second car is not yet clear.

Train Passing in Front of the Taj Mahal (Hidden)

Here, the artist gives his interpretation of the much-heard complaint of never getting to see the famous, majestic Taj Mahal of India. Some might inquire as to why he did a fabulously detailed drawing of the famed structure and then had it hidden by the train. The answer can be found in the fact that the artist is renowned as the "Master of the Unseen."

Snow-Covered Train in Siberia

A favorite of the minimalists, this strong illustration of the grandeur of the bleak Siberian Plain chills the viewer as he can only wonder how such a landscape can support life. The artist does want the viewer to know that he also drew 14 snow-covered huts along the tracks and a snow-white songbird with a broken left leg which is completely covered with the snow. Note the large white snowflakes, each painstakingly drawn to further illustrate the starkness of the Siberian winter and the suffering of the inhabitants of Mother Russia.

Train With Four Large, Hollowed-Out Snowballs

One of the artist's most poignant drawings, this depicts four large hollowed-out snowballs resting on the train's four railcars. Each hollowed-out snowball contains twin Inuit orphans, one of whom is gagging on rancid whale blubber. For reasons of privacy, drawings of the twins have been erased. It is not known why refrigeration of the whale blubber was a problem in the Arctic, or why the gagging reflex only affects orphaned Inuit twins.

Epilogue

I was told by my editor that this book so far includes many things that have happened and that I have done, but there is nothing about my inner thoughts, beliefs and current life.

Currently, I have been beset by a long list of medical problems such as two strokes, a heart attack, kidney failure, prostate and heart surgery, congestive heart failure, diabetes, vascular surgery in preparation for impending dialysis and last, but not least, sudden cardiac death. Yet here I am writing an autobiography.

I am well aware that I am late in the third act of a three-act play, and my days on this planet are numbered. How do I feel about that? As far as beliefs are concerned, I practice atheism religiously. I feel that I did not exist for billions of years, and it didn't seem to bother me. I will just return to my former state of non-existence. I have absolutely no problem with people believing in an after-life. I am in favor of people deriving peace, comfort and solace from their beliefs. However, there is a huge difference between believing and actually knowing. I readily admit that I don't know. Perhaps we go on to exist in another world. I DO NOT KNOW!!

However, one thing that I cannot explain did happen. Not long ago, my wife was extremely upset, had very jangled nerves, and was exhausted and tearful. Nothing I tried had any beneficial effect. I was at my wit's end as to what to do about the situation, which had become critical. I most definitely am not spiritual, but one night as I lay in bed feeling quite helpless, I heard, or thought I heard a voice saying, "Smother her with love." I do not know what the voice was or where it came from, other than that it did not seem to be from me.

Well, I really can't say that I smothered Joan with love, but I did try to assure her that I was always going to be there for her and that by working as a team we could and would make her situation more tolerable. Things improved quickly, and she was soon back to her normal self.

Did I really hear a voice?? I wonder.

These days I spend a lot of time reading, listening to music (classical and jazz), watching sports and doing nothing. I have attained a high level of expertise in doing nothing most of the day. The only problem with that is not being able to tell when I'm finished.

Of course I have made many mistakes along the way. I should have gotten my college degree much earlier. I wish I had been more mature when I married, just to name two.

As far as what grade I would give myself overall? I don't feel that I deserve an A or a C. I hereby award myself a B. To quote an old friend, "That ain't bad."

PHOTO GALLERY

Dad on his mother's lap, with his grandmother,
sister (Concetta) and brother (Dominic) back in
Calabria, Italy, probably about 1909.

Mom in Atlantic City, 1945

*Mom and
Dad with
Mickey and
me. (I'm on
the left.)*

Fixing the cellar door with Mickey.
Well, maybe <u>he</u> was fixing it.

1961

*I have no
idea what
cookout this
was. Looks
good, though.*

Paul (1965)
AFTER

Paul (1948)
BEFORE

Polka-Marion

Miss Joan Frances Marion, daughter of Mr. and Mrs. James N. Marion of White Plains, N.Y., was married September 2 to Paul James Polka, son of Mrs. James A. Polka of 152 Amelia Drive. The ceremony took place in St. Martin's Roman Catholic Church, New Hope.

Mr. Marion escorted his daughter, who wore a gown of ivory satin with appliqued Alencon lace motifs, on the empire waistline, elbow-length sleeves, scoop neckline and hem. A bow of ivory peau de soie and lace held her illusion veil. She carried an old-fashioned nosegay.

Miss Mary Joan Southard of Los Gatos, Calif., was the maid of honor and the brides-maid was Mrs. William W. Neall of Davidsonville, Md. Marguerite F. Marion and Helen E. Marion of Levittown, cousins of the bride, were flower girls.

Michael C. Polka of Slidell, La., served as best man, and James Polka of Levittown and Patrick Marion of White Plains were ushers.

The couple toured the

Joan and I were married September 2, 1967

MRS. POLKA

1973

At home, 1973

Oh don't you wish.!!

With son Brian at the pool next to our building at
Cambridge Hall Apartments, 1974.

*With the kids in their high school
band uniforms, 1985*

Playing pool at Mickey's house

*I was either contemplating the grandeur of nature
or nodding off.*

Radio City
Music Hall,
New York City,
1998

Modeling the
latest in ancient
Egyptian fashion
at the San Diego
Museum of Man,
2000

On a 2004 camping trip upstate with my brothers Mickey and Jim, we recreated a 1955 photo of Jim and me taken on our street in Pittston.

*Camping with
my brothers.
We rough it
well.*

*At a Pittston
High School
Class of '54
reunion*

*Modelling my
new vest,
Christmas 2009*

With Joan, Lizzie and Angel, Christmas 2009

For years, my kids ran a competition at Christmas to give me the tackiest possible snow globe, in honor of my tacky taste. These are the entries from 2009. Decisions, decisions....

With my daughter's close friend, Beth, and later singing off-key at a memorial for my father-in-law in 2010

More photos from the memorial.
Above: Carroll Scott, Joan and me
Below: Bridget, Joan, Brian, his wife Heather, and me

Christmas, 2010. The oven had stopped working, so I cooked the ham in the fireplace using my finely-honed survival skills. Son Brian pointed out the tags dangling from my mitts before I could catch on fire.

With Brian and Bridget at Bridget's wedding,
April 2011

"So a horse walks into a bar...."
August 2014

At home with Joan and Lizzie the dog
December 29, 2014

*At the local ice
cream shop,
after my "photo
shoot" for the
cover of this
book*

April 18, 2015

*Birthday barbecue,
May 26, 2017*

*Top picture, left to right: my
mother-in-law, Bridget, me,
and Bridget's husband, Dave.*

Joan took the picture.

Somehow, I got hoodwinked into making a video with my accordion in September, 2017.

Self-portrait while fooling around with photo software, 2017

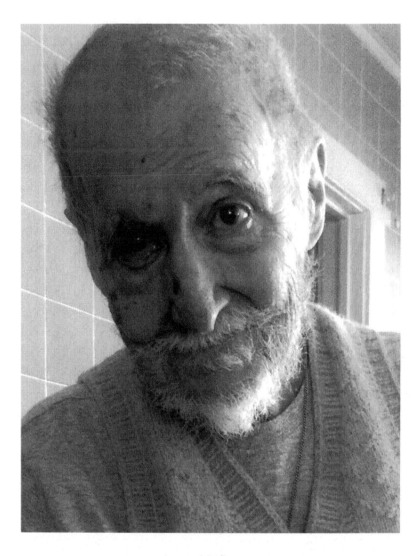

2017

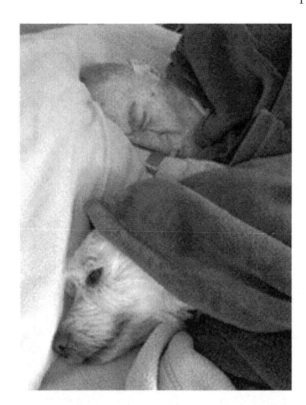

*Napping with
Lizzie
2018*

Editorial note:

As related earlier in these pages, Paul suffered sudden cardiac death in 2002. As he was recovering, he described what had happened as gentle, peaceful and painless, just a feeling of tiredness overcoming him. He talked often about his experience of having felt surrounded by intense love… but then having to come back despite wishing he could stay there.

On May 4, 2018, at about 9:30 PM, Paul suffered sudden cardiac death again. This time, he got to stay.

From your Vast Editorial Staff, goodnight, Dad. I love you.

Made in the USA
San Bernardino, CA
01 November 2018